LEGAL ARGUMENT

THE STRUCTURE AND LANGUAGE OF EFFECTIVE ADVOCACY

LAW SCHOOL ADVISORY BOARD

CO-CHAIRS

Howard P. Fink
Isadore & Ida Topper Professor of Law
Ohio State University
College of Law

Stephen A. Saltzburg
Howrey Professor of Trial Advocacy
George Washington University
National Law Center

MEMBERS

Charles B. Craver
Leroy S. Merrifield Research Professor of Law
George Washington University
National Law Center

Jane C. Ginsburg
Morton L. Janklow Professor of Literary and Artistic Property Law
Columbia University School of Law

Edward J. Imwinkelried
Professor of Law
University of California at Davis
School of Law

Daniel R. Mandelker
Howard A. Stamper Professor of Law
Washington University
School of Law

Mark V. Tushnet
Professor of Law
Georgetown University
National Law Center

LEGAL ARGUMENT

THE STRUCTURE AND LANGUAGE OF EFFECTIVE ADVOCACY

James A. Gardner
Professor of Law
Western New England College

THE MICHIE COMPANY
Law Publishers
CHARLOTTESVILLE, VIRGINIA

COPYRIGHT © 1993
BY
THE MICHIE COMPANY

Library of Congress Catalog Card Number: 93-80498

ISBN 1-55834-129-3

Printed in the United States of America

All rights reserved.

1149510

PREFACE

This book has a single purpose: to explain how lawyers construct legal arguments. It is meant to be a purely practical guide to the often mysterious process by which lawyers take the raw materials of litigation – cases, statutes, testimony, documents, common sense – and mold them into instruments of persuasive advocacy. In approaching this subject, I have tried to focus strictly on the fundamentals. The book is therefore concerned far less with the construction of arguments that are clever and elegant than with the crafting of arguments that are merely coherent and solidly grounded; such arguments are, after all, the real workhorses of legal practice. For this reason, the book probably has more in common with a home repair manual than with a legal treatise or a law review article; it is meant to offer step-by-step instructions on how to accomplish a thoroughly mundane, though highly necessary task.

Who needs a book like this? Certainly, many lawyers and law students can look at a collection of legal rules and evidence and see intuitively how to arrange them into a coherent argument. But my experience as a law teacher convinces me that a great many people who come to the practice of law lack this particular kind of intuition. For them, the construction of even the most straightforward legal argument can be an excruciating struggle, one that is especially frustrating because they understand the raw materials of the argument but are unable readily to articulate their understanding in a persuasive form. This book is for those people.

I must confess that there is a sense in which a book like this is quite absurd; it seeks to explain something that is so simple and so intuitive as to be quite possibly incapable of explanation. Making arguments is as basic to lawyers as running is to athletes. No one would attempt to write a book on how – "extend the left foot, keeping the knee slightly bent; contact the ground first with the heel and then smoothly roll the foot forward, all the while keeping your weight moving forward . . ." – yet that is more or less what I have done by trying to write a book for lawyers and law students about how to argue.

This might be a serious impediment for anyone who comes to the law completely ignorant of the craft of argument. In my view, however, no adult who has lived in our society and graduated from college – that is to say, no law student – can genuinely wholly lack the ability to mount an argument. More likely, people who have trouble crafting arguments stumble at no more than a few of the necessary steps. My hope is that such readers will, at some point in this book, experience a flash of recognition: "Oh," they will say to themselves, "*of course* that's how you do it." This possibility also makes the book of use even to those who make good arguments intuitively. By stating explicitly what the intuitive arguer understands only implicitly, the book may strengthen the intuitive arguer's skills or help him or her to work out especially challenging or complex arguments.

What I have said so far should make clear that the book is aimed primarily at law students, and most particularly at first year law students, although I hope it will be of use even to experienced practitioners who want to sharpen their argument skills. The book deals almost exclusively with written advocacy, primarily because the great bulk of most lawyers' advocacy (with the prominent exception of criminal lawyers) is written. Nevertheless, much of what is said here holds just as well for oral as for written argument. The book also focuses on advocacy in the lower courts, particularly in trial courts, again because that is where most lawyers spend most of their time, and because the differences between trial advocacy and appellate advocacy are comparatively minor.

One thing the book does not cover is research skills; it is by no means a comprehensive introduction to lawyering and it therefore assumes that its readers know how to round up the raw materials from which they will craft their arguments. The book also does not cover in any systematic way the subject of legal writing. To be sure, it is impossible to give a complete account of the methodology of legal argument without covering the ways in which legal arguments are reduced to writing, and the book devotes a lengthy chapter to this subject. Nevertheless, the book is not intended to be a guide to good legal writing, but a guide to the manipulation of legal concepts. There can be no doubt that a sure hand in the manipulation of the underlying concepts can only improve the quality of the written argument, but those who seek comprehensive advice on the elements of good legal writing should look elsewhere.

The book is organized into three parts. The first part sets out a general methodology for constructing legal arguments. This methodology centers on the use of syllogisms and the process of what I call "grounding" their premises. The second part focuses more closely on the construction of persuasive, well-grounded legal premises, and covers the effective integration of legal doctrine and evidence into the argument's structure. It then gives a detailed example of the construction of a complete legal argument from scratch, followed by a discussion of how to reduce legal arguments to written form and an illustration of that process. The final part of the book covers some miscellaneous considerations, including responding to arguments, common rhetorical techniques, and the ethical limits of argument.

A final warning is in order. This book provides a methodology for constructing legal arguments, but no methodology, in this discipline or any other, can ever be more than a reliable rule of thumb. A methodology can provide highly useful guidance to the initiate and the expert alike, but it is never a substitute for practiced judgment based on real experience. The true master of a craft knows when to deviate from the rules as well as when to follow them, when to cut corners and when to proceed strictly. The advice contained in this book should be taken in this spirit.

I want to take this opportunity to thank the many friends, relations, colleagues, and students whose encouragement made the writing of this book so pleasurable. For their assistance and useful comments on drafts of this work, special thanks are due to Lise Gelernter, Jay Mootz, Cathy Lanctot, Angelo Grima, Dee DeGeiso, the students in my Legal Argument class, the members of the Western New England College School of Law National Moot Court team, and my many colleagues who attended the faculty forum at which I presented a draft.

JAG
Springfield, Mass.
May 27, 1993

SUMMARY TABLE OF CONTENTS

Page

Preface v
Table of Contents xi

PART I. THE BASIC METHOD

CHAPTER 1. THE SYLLOGISM MODEL 3
CHAPTER 2. DETERMINING YOUR CONCLUSION FROM YOUR POSITION 15
CHAPTER 3. BUILDING THE PREMISES 27
CHAPTER 4. GROUNDING THE PREMISES 39

PART II. ELEMENTS OF PERSUASIVE LEGAL ARGUMENT

CHAPTER 5. THE MAJOR PREMISE 53
CHAPTER 6. THE MINOR PREMISE 71
CHAPTER 7. SUMMARY OF THE METHOD (A STEP-BY-STEP ANALYSIS) 93
CHAPTER 8. PUTTING TOGETHER A COMPLETE ARGUMENT 97
CHAPTER 9. WRITING A LEGAL ARGUMENT 109

PART III. ADDITIONAL CONSIDERATIONS

CHAPTER 10. SPECIAL PROBLEMS 131
CHAPTER 11. RESPONDING TO ARGUMENTS 139
CHAPTER 12. SOME COMMON RHETORICAL TECHNIQUES 151
CHAPTER 13. THE ETHICAL LIMITS OF ARGUMENT 161

TABLE OF CONTENTS

Page

Preface v
Summary Table of Contents ix

PART I. THE BASIC METHOD

CHAPTER 1. THE SYLLOGISM MODEL 3
§ 1.1. Introduction 3
§ 1.2. Syllogisms 4
§ 1.3. The Power of Syllogistic Reasoning 6
§ 1.4. Legal Arguments as Syllogisms 8
§ 1.5. The Incompleteness of the Analogy Approach 10

CHAPTER 2. DETERMINING YOUR CONCLUSION FROM YOUR POSITION 15
§ 2.1. What Should You Argue? 15
§ 2.2. The Elements of Presumptive Position 16
§ 2.3. The Adversary System: A Sorting Mechanism 17
§ 2.4. Determining Your Presumptive Positions 19
§ 2.5. Actual Positions 21
§ 2.6. The Core Position: Relief 22
§ 2.6.1. Ultimate Relief in the Case 22
§ 2.6.2. Relief Sought in a Motion 23
§ 2.7. Converting Positions Into Syllogisms 24
§ 2.8. The Need to Commit to a Position 25

CHAPTER 3. BUILDING THE PREMISES 27
§ 3.1. Introduction 27
§ 3.2. The Premises Must Yield the Desired Conclusion 27
§ 3.3. All Terms Must Match 28
§ 3.4. The Specification of Any Two Terms Specifies the Third 31

Page
§ 3.5. The Premises Must Be True 32
§ 3.6. A Recursive Process 33
§ 3.7. The Indeterminacy of Law 37

CHAPTER 4. GROUNDING THE PREMISES 39
§ 4.1. The Requirement of Grounding 39
§ 4.2. Directly Grounded Premises 41
§ 4.3. Indirect Grounding Through Nested Syllogisms 42
§ 4.4. Multiple Grounding 47
§ 4.5. Grounding in Controversial First Principles .. 48

PART II. ELEMENTS OF PERSUASIVE LEGAL ARGUMENT

CHAPTER 5. THE MAJOR PREMISE 53
§ 5.1. Introduction 53
§ 5.2. The Basic Strategy 54
§ 5.3. Establishing Certainty of Authoritativeness ... 55
§ 5.3.1. Sources of Authority 55
§ 5.3.2. Direct Grounding in Targeted Authority 56
§ 5.3.3. Indirect Grounding of the Major Premise 60
§ 5.4. Establishing Certainty in Content 63
§ 5.4.1. Tests 63
§ 5.4.2. Step Analysis 67
§ 5.4.3. Factor Analysis 68
§ 5.4.4. A Factor Analysis Can Always Be Extracted 69
§ 5.4.5. The Utility of Lower Court Decisions ... 70

Page

CHAPTER 6. THE MINOR PREMISE 71
§ 6.1. Introduction 71
§ 6.2. Establishing Certainty of Authoritativeness ... 72
§ 6.2.1. Ground Factual Assertions in Evidence 72
§ 6.2.2. Types of Evidence 75
§ 6.2.3. Appeals to Common Sense 76
§ 6.3. Establish Certainty of Content By Using Brute Facts 77
§ 6.3.1. Brute Facts and Compound Facts 77
§ 6.3.2. Break Down Compound Facts Into Brute Facts 79
§ 6.4. Elaborate Key Legal Terms 81
§ 6.4.1. Legal Aspects of the Minor Premise 81
§ 6.4.2. Identify the Key Terms 82
§ 6.4.3. Tell the Judge: "Here's How You Know It When You See It" 83
§ 6.5. Conclusory Argument 88
§ 6.6. A Grounded Minor Premise Guides Factual Development 92

CHAPTER 7. SUMMARY OF THE METHOD (A STEP-BY-STEP ANALYSIS) 93

CHAPTER 8. PUTTING TOGETHER A COMPLETE ARGUMENT 97
§ 8.1. Introduction 97
§ 8.2. The Facts 97
§ 8.3. The Law 98
§ 8.4. The Argument 101

CHAPTER 9. WRITING A LEGAL ARGUMENT 109
§ 9.1. A Formula For Writing Arguments 109
§ 9.2. Elements of the Formula 110

Page
§ 9.2.1. The Set-Up 110
§ 9.2.2. Setting Out the Law 113
§ 9.2.3. Apply the Law to the Facts 116
§ 9.2.4. Bolster With Analogous Precedent 119
§ 9.3. Clarity Always Takes Precedence 119
§ 9.4. An Example of Reducing an Argument to Writing 120
§ 9.4.1. The Outline 120
§ 9.4.2. The Brief 121

PART III. ADDITIONAL CONSIDERATIONS

CHAPTER 10. SPECIAL PROBLEMS 131
§ 10.1. The Big Case 131
§ 10.2. No Controlling Authority 133
§ 10.2.1. The Nature of the Problem 133
§ 10.2.2. Grounding the Argument in First Principles 134
§ 10.2.3. Justice, Morality, and Policy 136
§ 10.3. Balanced Legal Writing 137

CHAPTER 11. RESPONDING TO ARGUMENTS ... 139
§ 11.1. Affirmative and Responsive Arguments 139
§ 11.2. Treat Your Opponent's Arguments Respectfully 141
§ 11.3. Three Ways to Respond 142
§ 11.3.1. Denial 142
§ 11.3.2. Shifting Ground: Confession and Avoidance 145
§ 11.3.3. Ignoring Arguments 147
§ 11.4. Organizing Responses 148

Page

CHAPTER 12. SOME COMMON RHETORICAL TECHNIQUES . . . 151
§ 12.1. The "Shared Struggle" . . . 151
§ 12.2. Use the Language of Fallback Arguments . . 153
§ 12.3. The Persuasiveness of Detail . . . 154
§ 12.4. Attack the Opponent, Not the Court . . . 155
§ 12.5. Calling Attention to the Legal Standard . . . 156
§ 12.6. Providing the Court With Escape Routes . . . 159

CHAPTER 13. THE ETHICAL LIMITS OF ARGUMENT . . . 161
§ 13.1. The Ethical Dilemma . . . 161
§ 13.2. Official Constraints . . . 162
§ 13.3. Good Faith . . . 163
§ 13.3.1. Bad Faith: It's False . . . 164
§ 13.3.2. Bad Faith: No One Could Believe It . . 164
§ 13.3.3. Good Faith: Winners and Losers . . . 165
§ 13.3.4. Maintaining Your Sense of Good Faith . . . 166
§ 13.4. The Settlement Option . . . 167

NOTE ON CASE CITATIONS

Most of the "cases" cited in the text as examples are fictional, and thus no full citation has been provided. A few of the cases and all of the statutes mentioned are genuine, but full citations have been omitted to avoid cluttering up the text. It should go without saying that lawyers submitting written work to courts should always provide full citations for every case, statute or other source they mention.

PART I
THE BASIC METHOD

Chapter 1

THE SYLLOGISM MODEL

§ 1.1. Introduction.
§ 1.2. Syllogisms.
§ 1.3. The Power of Syllogistic Reasoning.
§ 1.4. Legal Arguments as Syllogisms.
§ 1.5. The Incompleteness of the Analogy Approach.

§ 1.1. Introduction.

Every legal advocate faces the challenge of creating order out of chaos. The advocate must take an undisciplined mass of information and argument and reshape it into a tool capable of converting the most skeptical decision maker to the advocate's point of view. How to accomplish this daunting feat is the subject of this book.

Effective advocacy does not come naturally to many. Most people do not think in an orderly way. Thoughts do not traverse the mind like a military parade, four abreast in neat rows and columns; they race in and out of consciousness from every direction and in no obvious order. Not surprisingly, most people argue the way they think — haphazardly, without clear structure, and often without recognizing or consciously understanding the logical connections between their own arguments and contentions.

Beginning law students are often told that the proper way to present a legal argument is: "set out the law and then apply it to the facts." This advice is sound as far as it goes; unfortunately it does not go very far, and it provides little in the way of concrete guidance. This book aims to fill that gap by offering a systematic method for the construction of persuasive legal arguments.

The centerpiece of the method presented in the following pages is the *syllogism,* and the book's thesis can be simply stated: all legal argument should be in the form of syllogisms. The term *syllogism* will doubtless strike fear into the hearts of many lawyers and law students; it looks like a mathematical term, and lawyers are notorious for their disdain of all things mathematical. Lawyers like to see the law as warm, fuzzy, humanistic; to them, the law is not the stuff of hard-edged logic, nor is it amenable to mathematical manipulation.

All this is true, of course – the law *is* fuzzy and humanistic, and it can be as illogical as the humans who create it. The trick to persuasive legal argument, however, is to take an indistinct subject and make it *seem* mathematical. Remember that the judge is every bit as despondent as the advocate when confronted with the chaotic thicket of law and facts in any given case. Indeed, the judge wants nothing more than to be led out of this jungle by a confident, reliable guide – "Right this way, Your Honor. Watch out for that snake, Your Honor."

Syllogistic argument provides the requisite appearance of certainty. It makes the outcome of a case seem as certain and as mechanical as the output of a mathematical equation, and it achieves this effect not by employing actual mathematical operations, but, paradoxically, by exploiting human intuition.

§ 1.2. Syllogisms.

A syllogism is a statement of logical relationship. The typical syllogism has three parts:

1. The *major premise,* usually a broad statement of general applicability;
2. The *minor premise,* usually a narrower statement of particular applicability that is related in some way to the major premise; and
3. The *conclusion,* the logical consequence of the major and minor premises.

A classic example of a syllogism which has been studied by students for centuries follows:

1. All men are mortal.
2. Socrates is a man.
3. Therefore, Socrates is mortal.

Two features of this syllogism are important for our purposes. First, notice the form of the premises. The major premise, "All men are mortal," states a general rule or proposition describing the relationship of men to mortality. The rule is couched so as to apply to all men at all times; by its terms, it admits of no exception. The minor premise, in contrast, is much narrower in focus. The statement, "Socrates is a man," is specific and concrete; it does not address broad and abstract principles, but rather a particular person, whom it merely describes.

Second, notice the way the conclusion follows logically from the premises. If all men are mortal, and if Socrates is a man, then we do not need to be logicians to figure out that Socrates must be mortal. Intuition alone not only furnishes the conclusion of the syllogism, but does so with a force amounting to compulsion.

Below are some other examples of syllogisms.

1. Books printed on paper will eventually decay.
2. This book is printed on paper.
3. Therefore, this book will eventually decay.

1. One American dollar is equivalent to five French francs.
2. I have one American dollar.
3. Therefore, I have the equivalent of five French francs.

1. No car that breaks down all the time is a good car.
2. Janet's car breaks down all the time.
3. Therefore, Janet's car is not a good car.

§ 1.3. The Power of Syllogistic Reasoning.

When presented with the properly framed major and minor premises of a syllogism, the human mind seems to produce the conclusion without any additional prompting. Moreover, the mind recognizes the conclusion to be of such compelling force that the conclusion simply cannot be denied. It is impossible to agree that all men are mortal and that Socrates is a man, yet deny that Socrates is mortal; to do so is to speak nonsense. Why is this? What accounts for the power of syllogistic reasoning?

Essentially, the syllogism is nothing more than an application in words of the basic mathematical principle of *transitivity,* a principle familiar to all schoolchildren (but frequently forgotten by adults). The principle of transitivity states: if $A = B$, and $B = C$, then $A = C$; that is, if two things are equal to the same thing, then they are equal to each other.

The terms of a syllogism correspond to the terms of the transitivity principle. To see this, reconsider the Socrates example, assigning the variable A to Socrates, the variable B to men, and the variable C to mortality:

1.	All men [B] are mortal [C].	$B = C$
2.	Socrates [A] is a man [B].	$A = B$
3.	Thus, Socrates [A] is mortal [C].	$A = C$

The syllogism, then, says nothing more than that two things (Socrates and mortals) equivalent to the same thing (men) are equivalent to each other.[1]

Beyond this, of course, there is no further explanation for the power of syllogistic reasoning. The transitivity principle is an axiom; it is something we believe, but cannot exactly prove. Its appeal derives from its reflection of what we take to be a basic fact about the universe we live in. We cannot even begin to comprehend what the world would be like if the principle of transitivity did not hold – if A were equal to B, and B were equal to C, but somehow A were *not* also equal to C. That is why it seems insane to try to deny the conclusion of a properly framed syllogism; to deny the syllogism's conclusion is to deny the world itself as we understand it.

For the advocate, the logical and mathematical foundations of the syllogism make it an awesomely powerful tool of persuasion. This is so for one very simple reason: when you present an argument in the form of a syllogism, *if your listeners accept your premises, then they MUST accept your conclusion.* Once your premises are accepted, the logical

---

[1]The foregoing explanation is probably as much as (and possibly more than) most students and lawyers will need. Nevertheless, at the risk of belaboring the mathematical basis of syllogistic reasoning, some readers may recognize that this particular syllogism is more accurately viewed as an application of set theory. In other words, the set of men is a subset of the set of mortals (B ϵ C); Socrates is a member of the set of men (A ϵ B); therefore, Socrates is a member of the set of mortals (A ϵ C). This relationship is shown in the diagram.

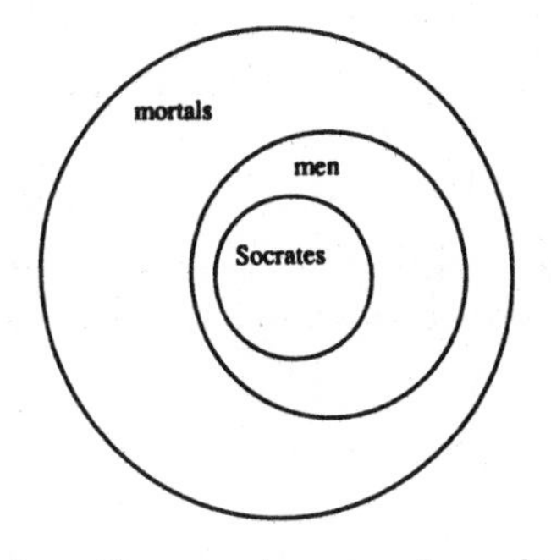

force of the syllogism precludes any subsequent denial of the conclusion toward which the syllogism inexorably drives; one who has agreed to the premises is trapped.

This does not mean, of course, that one who presents an argument in the form of a syllogism can never be refuted. It does mean, however, that the only way to refute a syllogistic argument is to dispute its premises, not its conclusion; a well-framed syllogism will always be internally consistent and irrefutable on its own terms. Consider the following example:

1. All orbiting bodies are made of green cheese.
2. The moon is an orbiting body.
3. Therefore, the moon is made of green cheese.

On its own terms, this syllogism is logical; however, the internal logic and consistency of the syllogism do not make it true. This syllogism is false because the major premise is false, not because of any defect in its structure. Even the most logical applications of false premises inevitably yield false conclusions. Thus, one who wishes to dispute the conclusion of a proper syllogism cannot successfully do so by arguing that the conclusion does not flow logically from the premises. The only available strategy is to contest the premises.[2]

§ 1.4. Legal Arguments as Syllogisms.

The power of syllogistic argument leads to the only significant rule about crafting legal arguments: *every good legal argument is cast in the form of a syllogism.*

When a legal argument is cast as a syllogism, it generally takes the following form. The major premise is a statement

[2]It is also possible to construct a structurally improper syllogism. This type of error is discussed more fully in § 11.3.1.

of the *law*; it is, like most major premises, a general proposition of general applicability. The minor premise of a legal syllogism is a proposition concerning the *application* of the law to the particular circumstances of the case at hand. The conclusion, of course, derives from the major and minor premises.

Following are some examples of legal arguments which are cast in the form of syllogisms:

1. In order to be enforceable, a contract must be supported by consideration.
2. The contract between Tim and Mary is not supported by consideration.
3. Therefore, the contract between Tim and Mary is not enforceable.

1. Federal courts have diversity jurisdiction only over claims exceeding $50,000.
2. Sonia's personal injury claim against Alpha Car Rental exceeds $50,000.
3. Therefore, federal courts have diversity jurisdiction over Sonia's personal injury claim against Alpha.

1. The Equal Protection Clause prohibits intentional discrimination on the basis of race.
2. Laws barring blacks from serving on juries constitute intentional discrimination based on race.
3. Therefore, the Equal Protection Clause prohibits laws barring blacks from serving on juries.

Notice from these examples how particularly well suited legal arguments are to the syllogism format. It is often said that a legal argument consists of nothing more than setting out the law and then applying it to the facts of the case. That is precisely what a syllogistic legal argument does. The major premise sets out a proposition of law. The minor premise then applies that legal proposition to the facts and circumstances of a particular conflict. The conclusion flows from the application of law to fact.

§ 1.5. The Incompleteness of the Analogy Approach.

Common wisdom has it that legal reasoning proceeds by analogy.[3] This maxim is true in an important way, but it is nevertheless a very misleading way to look at legal argument, and is probably responsible for many a poorly crafted and confusing argument.

Like a syllogism, an analogy is a statement of logical relationship. An analogy compares two things and declares that they are alike: A is like B, C is like D. Analogies can also compare degrees of similarity: A is like B, and A is also like C, but A is more like B than it is like C.

The purpose of an analogy in legal reasoning is to help the decision maker assign disparate things to their proper legal categories. For example, consider the sale of a house. The law generally presumes that the sellers do not intend to sell their *personal property* (or *personalty*), but that they do intend to sell the *fixtures* along with the house. Thus, if an article falls within the category of personal property the sellers may remove it, but if the article falls into the fixture category the law presumes that it was sold along with the house.

Suppose we know from prior cases that a bathtub is a fixture and a table is personalty. Now consider a wood stove: is it a fixture or personalty? Like a bathtub, a wood stove is large and heavy; but, like a table, a wood stove can be moved without disturbing the structural integrity of the

[3] The leading work is still Edward H. Levi, *An Introduction to Legal Reasoning* (1949).

house. Analogical legal reasoning asks whether a wood stove is more like a bathtub than it is like a table.

While analogies are thus useful in legal *reasoning,* they play a more limited role in legal *argument.* The obvious inadequacy of the use of analogy in constructing a legal argument is an analogy's inability to answer the question, "so what?" Suppose I tell you: "A wood stove is more like a bathtub than it is like a table." You say: "All right, but so what?" The analogy itself supplies no answer to this challenge. Of course, the answer is clear enough: the fact that a wood stove is more like a bathtub than it is like a table is legally significant because it means that a wood stove is a fixture that the law presumes is sold along with the house. Notice, however, that the relevant legal *argument* does not derive from the analogy, but from an implicit syllogism:

1. Fixtures stay with the house.
2. A wood stove is a fixture.
3. Therefore, a wood stove stays with the house.

It takes a syllogism to provide the answer to the "so what" challenge. That is, the logical force of an analogy comes from the syllogism to which it contributes, not from the persuasiveness of the analogy itself. Or, put another way, an analogy is a way of defending a premise of a syllogism; by itself, it is not an argument but merely a small piece of an argument.

When an advocate loses sight of the limited role of analogies and relies on analogies rather than on the syllogisms of which they are implicit parts, the result is often a lengthy, unfocused series of case descriptions. Such arguments, well known to all teachers of first year law students, generally go something like this:

> This case is like *Allen v. Biggs*. In *Allen v. Biggs,* the plaintiff bought a house that contained a large, ornate chandelier in the front entry. Upon taking possession of the house, the plaintiff found the chandelier had been removed and subsequently sued for its return. The court ruled for the plaintiff, holding that a "large, bulky object" that was "physically connected to the structure" was a fixture. Also analogous is *Charles v. Dupree,* where the sellers had removed wall-to-wall carpeting throughout the house and the court likewise held that the removed object was a fixture. However, this case is easily distinguished from *Edwards v. Fitzpatrick*. There, the defendant removed a refrigerator, which the court held to be a fixture. However, the property at issue in *Edwards* was an apartment, and it is customary for apartment dwellers to leave large appliances behind. This case, in contrast, concerns a free-standing house.

These descriptions are often excruciatingly detailed, involving multiple cases, parties and claims. But at the end of it all, the reader usually asks, "so what?" The "so what" challenge can only be answered by reformulating the argument into a syllogism.

1. The rule of *Allen v. Biggs* and *Charles v. Dupree* applies in cases concerning large, bulky objects that are physically connected to a structure.
2. This case concerns a large, bulky object (a wood stove) that is physically connected to a structure.
3. Therefore, the rule of *Allen v. Biggs* and *Charles v. Dupree* applies in this case.

The analogies between the case at hand and the cases cited as precedent serve only the secondary function of *supporting* the premises of this syllogism. Thus, the analogy is not the argument; the syllogism is the argument.

Chapter 2

DETERMINING YOUR CONCLUSION FROM YOUR POSITION

§ 2.1. What Should You Argue?
§ 2.2. The Elements of Presumptive Position.
§ 2.3. The Adversary System: A Sorting Mechanism.
§ 2.4. Determining Your Presumptive Positions.
§ 2.5. Actual Positions.
§ 2.6. The Core Position: Relief.
  § 2.6.1. Ultimate Relief in the Case.
  § 2.6.2. Relief Sought in a Motion.
§ 2.7. Converting Positions Into Syllogisms.
§ 2.8. The Need to Commit to a Position.

§ 2.1. What Should You Argue?

The rule that a legal argument should be in the form of a syllogism says nothing at all about the content of that syllogism. How, then, does the advocate formulate a syllogism that will actually persuade a judge to rule favorably in a real case?

For an advocate to examine every combination of premises and conclusions potentially relevant to a particular case, searching for the best and most persuasive syllogistic argument, would be a hopeless task. Fortunately, the choices available to an advocate are quite constrained, so the number of syllogisms suitable for use in any given case is limited.

Unlike a philosopher, a legal advocate does not deal with open-ended questions, nor does the advocate approach a legal problem with an open mind. The need to make a legal argument never arises in a vacuum; it arises only in the context of a specific case, in which specific parties seek specific judicial relief. This intrinsic property of advocacy gives the advocate a unique advantage over less directed thinkers: the advocate knows the answers to all relevant questions *before* commencing his or her inquiries. This is so for one simple reason: the advocate always represents the interests of a particular party, and the advocate's goal is to help that party achieve victory in a particular legal dispute. Consequently, from the entire universe of available arguments, the advocate is entitled to contemplate only those few arguments that will help the client *win*. Indeed, the initial question facing any advocate is never "What *should* I argue?" but rather "What *must* I argue in order to win this case?"

Fair enough. But how does the advocate know what arguments must be made to win the case, and how should these arguments be converted into syllogistic form? The answer to both these questions is provided by the *position*. The advocate's position not only determines the content of the legal arguments that the advocate must make, but also provides the advocate with the conclusion to every syllogism that he or she may wish to present. Knowing a conclusion, the advocate may construct a syllogism by working backward from the predetermined conclusion, rather than haphazardly discovering the conclusion by experimenting with potential premises.

Isolation of the appropriate set of syllogism conclusions is a two-step process. First, the advocate must generate a set of *presumptive positions*. These positions are the ones that have the potential to help the advocate win. Second, the advocate evaluates this set of presumptive positions and from it selects the *actual positions* to be used in the litigation.

§ 2.2. The Elements of Presumptive Position.

As an advocate, your presumptive position in any case is a function of two factors: (1) your client's *alignment* in the case, and (2) any relevant *legal principles*. The client's alignment is simply his or her party status – basically, plaintiff or defendant.[4] The relevant legal principles are simply those rules of law that might conceivably apply to the case. Some examples of legal principles that might be relevant to a case are: negligence, assumption of risk, admissibility of evidence, offer and acceptance, federal question jurisdiction, due process, or separation of powers.

At this early stage in the construction of the argument, it is not even necessary to decide whether a particular area of law actually applies to the case, or which way any particular legal question is likely to be resolved. It is enough to know that certain legal principles *might* be relevant to resolution of the case.

§ 2.3. The Adversary System: A Sorting Mechanism.

Once you have identified your alignment in the case and some potentially relevant legal principles, you can generate a set of presumptive positions by feeding this data, so to speak, into the sorting mechanism provided by the *adversary system*.

All legal cases in our society are conducted according to the adversary system. Under that system, parties with opposing interests come before a court for resolution of their dispute. Each party presents its own side of the case as forcefully as possible, and then the judge chooses between them. The theory behind the adversary system is that the court is best able to discern the truth by observing the clash of starkly opposing viewpoints. In any event, an

---

[4] Technically, a litigant may hold a status other than that of plaintiff or defendant; for example, one can be an intervenor, a third-party defendant, or a counterclaimant. However, all parties ultimately end up aligned with the plaintiff or defendant, or can be considered a plaintiff or defendant with respect to some other party.

indispensable element of any case in our system is that the parties must always be adverse; if they agree with each other, there is no dispute requiring resolution, and hence no case to be decided.

The requirement of party adversity provides the advocate with a fail-safe method for determining precisely which arguments the parties in any case will presumptively wish to make. It all boils down to this: a plaintiff is always *for* anything that leads to the liability of the defendant, and the defendant is always *against* anything that leads to liability. It makes no difference what it is that leads to liability; it could be a legal principle, a controlling precedent, a factual finding, or anything else – whatever it is, the plaintiff is always *for* it, and the defendant is always *against* it.

Note that the parties *must* make these arguments; they simply have no choice in the matter. If a plaintiff wants to win, it must make only those arguments that lead to imposition of liability on the defendant, and it must oppose any arguments made by the defendant against liability. If the plaintiff fails to make the arguments that lead to the defendant's liability, it will fail to carry its burden of persuasion and will lose. If the plaintiff fails to oppose the defendant's dispositive arguments it will also lose because a court will usually accept the defendant's arguments if they are unopposed.

Conversely, the defendant must oppose any argument made by the plaintiff that leads to the defendant's liability. If the defendant fails to do so, the plaintiff's complaint will be unopposed and the defendant will lose. Likewise, the defendant must advance affirmatively any arguments leading to exoneration.

These simple deductions from the nature of the adversary system provide a convenient sorting mechanism that takes a party's alignment and the relevant legal principles and converts them into the party's positions in the case.

§ 2.4. Determining Your Presumptive Positions.

Suppose your client is the plaintiff in a contract dispute. If you know that much, you already know enough to begin formulating your presumptive positions in the case: you know your client's alignment in the case (plaintiff) and you know the relevant legal principles (contract law). All you need to do is feed this information into the adversary system.

We know from the adversary system that the plaintiff, your client, must argue *for* anything that could lead to the imposition of liability on the defendant. What could lead to contractual liability? The first requirement is certainly the existence of a contract. Thus, your client's presumptive position in the case must be: There *was* a contract. The plaintiff in a contractual dispute must take this position or lose the case. Conversely, the defendant's presumptive position in the case on this issue must be: There was *not* a contract.

The more you know about the relevant law, the greater the detail with which you can flesh out your presumptive positions. For example, assume that the elements of a valid contract are: offer, acceptance, and consideration. What is the plaintiff's position on each of these sub-issues? Clearly, if you want to win for your client you must argue that (1) there *was* an offer; (2) the defendant *did* accept it; and (3) the contract *was* supported by consideration. If you fail to take these positions, you cannot win the case. The defendant, of course, presumptively must respond that (1) there was *no* offer; (2) if there was an offer, the defendant did *not* accept it; and (3) the alleged contract was *not* supported by consideration.

Suppose the remedy is an issue because your client wants specific performance. Again, the adversary system determines the presumptive positions of the parties: the plaintiff presumptively must argue that specific performance *is* an appropriate remedy under the circumstances, and the defendant presumptively must argue that specific performance is *not* appropriate.

We can determine the parties' positions in other types of cases as well. Consider a personal injury case based on negligence.

Legal issue	**Plaintiff's presumptive position**	**Defendant's presumptive position**
Negligence	D was negligent	D was not negligent
Duty	D owed P a duty of care	D did not owe P a duty of care
Breach	D breached its duty	D did not breach any duty
Injury	P was injured	P was not injured
Causation	D's breach caused P's injury	D's breach did not cause P's injury
Assumption of risk	P did not assume the risk	P assumed the risk
Contributory negligence	P was not contributorily negligent	P was contributorily negligent

It is possible to go on and on. A plaintiff is always presumptively *for* the existence of jurisdiction, a defendant always presumptively *against* it. A plaintiff is always *for* the admissibility of its own evidence and presumptively *against* the admissibility of the defendant's evidence (and vice versa for the defendant). In a constitutional case, a plaintiff is always presumptively *for* a demanding standard of judicial review and a defendant is always presumptively *against* it.

Note how mechanical this process is, and how little discretion the advocate actually has. Your client's party alignment is fixed, and so are the requirements of the adversary system. Virtually the only aspect of the process over which the advocate has any control is in deciding what legal principles are relevant to the case. But even then, once any party has concluded that some legal issue is relevant, the parties' positions on that issue are not discretionary: the plaintiff *must* take the position that leads to liability and the defendant *must* take the position that defeats liability.

§2.5. Actual Positions.

Once the set of presumptive positions has been generated, the advocate must select from that set the group of actual positions for use in the case. It is often possible for the advocate to adopt the entire set of presumptive positions for actual use, but sometimes certain presumptive positions must be discarded.

The most common defect in a presumptive position that disqualifies it for use in a real case is that it is false. For example, suppose you represent the defendant in a negligence suit. Two elements of tort liability are: the plaintiff must have suffered an injury, and the defendant must have caused the injury. It follows that in order to defend your client, you will want to take these two positions, presumptively, among others: (1) the plaintiff was *not* injured; (2) even if the plaintiff was injured, the defendant did *not* cause the injury.

If you want to make the first of these two arguments, you will have to be able to show that the plaintiff really was not injured – that he or she is a faker and a liar. Now it sometimes happens that plaintiffs fake injuries, or exaggerate the extent of their injuries, in which case you could argue to the court that the plaintiff was not really injured at all. In most cases, however, investigation will reveal that the plaintiff really *was* injured and it is simply impossible credibly or ethically to argue otherwise. In these cases, the advocate has no choice but to abandon such a presumptive position as indefensible and concentrate on other, stronger positions, such as the causation issue. Thus, in this example, the defendant would admit that the plaintiff was injured, but would argue (again, if possible) that the plaintiff's injury was not caused by the actions of the defendant.

Presumptive positions can also be discarded even if they are not outright falsehoods. Even a true presumptive position may be unsuitable for use in litigation if it is unpersuasive, too complex to explain succinctly to a jury, or too expensive to prove. The important point to keep in mind is that not every position needs to be or even can be defended with a good argument. Much more will be said about the intricacies of argument selection in Chapter 13, which discusses the ethical limits of argument.

§ 2.6. The Core Position: Relief.

§ 2.6.1. Ultimate Relief in the Case.

Lawyers constantly wrangle over the law and the facts, and in complex litigation this wrangling can go on for years. Nevertheless, few lawsuits are really about the law and the facts. Rather, the ultimate subject of almost every lawsuit is *relief*. Whether the relief requested is money, specific performance, an injunction, or a declaration, in every case the plaintiff claims to be entitled to certain relief and the defendant denies it. In all other disputes, the parties merely jockey for position in the ultimate contest over this most fundamental disagreement.

As a result, the advocate absolutely must take a position, in every case, on the plaintiff's entitlement to relief. This position serves as the core of the parties' arguments, the one piece of the case that they can never surrender no matter how many of their legal and factual positions they may eventually be forced to abandon.

As with any position, a party's position on relief is driven by the party's alignment. The plaintiff must of course take the position that it is entitled to all the requested relief. The defendant, in contrast, must ordinarily deny that the plaintiff is entitled to any relief whatsoever. If a party is unable to adopt the appropriate position on relief for actual use in the case, then that party has no choice but to settle.

Because of its importance, a party's position on the relief should always be the starting point for the party's construction of a legal argument. All other positions are only means of supporting that core position.

§2.6.2. Relief Sought in a Motion.

Not every legal argument concerns the ultimate merits of the lawsuit. Indeed, the majority of legal arguments are addressed to issues that are only intermediate steps on the road to the ultimate relief sought in the case. These issues come up most often in *motions* – motions to dismiss, motions for summary judgment, motions to compel discovery, motions to exclude evidence, and many others.

Although the advocate must formulate and maintain a position on the ultimate relief sought by the plaintiff in every case, whenever a party requests specific relief in a motion, the advocate must formulate a position on that relief as well. Naturally, if your client is the movant, your position must be that your client is entitled to the relief sought; if the other party has moved, your position must be that the relief sought in the motion must be denied. This position will be the centerpiece of your legal arguments relating to the motion.

§ 2.7. Converting Positions Into Syllogisms.

Once you have determined your actual position or positions in the case, you can take the first step toward constructing the syllogisms by which you will present your arguments to the court. Specifically, *each position should be converted to the conclusion of a syllogistic argument.*

Consider again a contract case in which the plaintiff seeks enforcement of a contract. Starting with the question of relief, we might begin to construct a syllogism as follows:

1.
2.
3. Therefore, the plaintiff is entitled to damages.

Because contract law applies to this case, we might also consider a syllogism like the following:

1.
2.
3. Therefore, there was a valid contract.

In addition, we might want to consider the following syllogisms based on the more detailed positions we developed in § 2.4:

1.
2.
3. Therefore, the plaintiff made a valid offer.

1.
2.
3. Therefore, the defendant accepted plaintiff's offer.

1.
2.
3. Therefore, the contract was supported by consideration.

How to complete these syllogisms by constructing the premises is the subject of Chapters 3 through 6.

§ 2.8. The Need to Commit to a Position.

It should be obvious from the preceding discussion that every advocate must commit firmly to a position in every case. The adversary system demands a genuine conflict between the parties; this is impossible when any party is equivocal about its position. Moreover, effective legal argument itself demands that the advocate take a clearly defined position in order to construct a coherent syllogism.

Unfortunately, law students often seem reluctant to commit themselves to a position, even when they are cast as advocates whose positions are fully determined by their clients' interests. Perhaps this is because law students are taught to see all sides of an issue, or because they are reluctant to foreclose any legal options, or because they don't fully believe in the positions they must take. Whatever the cause, the tendency to waffle about one's position is incompatible with effective advocacy, and must be resisted. If your client is the plaintiff in a contract dispute, there *must* have been a contract if your client is to prevail. The advocate does not have the luxury of acting as though the existence of a contract is an open question, or that it seems more likely than not; for the advocate, there *was* a contract, and all arguments leading to that conclusion are correct just as surely as all arguments leading to any other conclusion are wrong.

The unpleasant truth is that there is no such thing as risk-free litigation. To win, you must risk losing. Only by differentiating your position from that of your opponent can you create the conditions under which the court can rule for you and against your opponent. But taking that step also creates the conditions under which the court can rule for your opponent instead of you. Making legal arguments necessarily involves climbing out on a limb. The trick is to pick the strongest limb – or, if that is impossible, to make your limb *look* stronger than your opponent's.

Chapter 3

BUILDING THE PREMISES

§ 3.1. Introduction.
§ 3.2. The Premises Must Yield the Desired Conclusion.
§ 3.3. All Terms Must Match.
§ 3.4. The Specification of Any Two Terms Specifies the Third.
§ 3.5. The Premises Must Be True.
§ 3.6. A Recursive Process.
§ 3.7. The Indeterminacy of Law.

§ 3.1. Introduction.

Once you have determined your position in a case and have converted that position into the conclusion of a syllogism, the next step is to construct the rest of the argument by building the premises of the syllogism. How is this accomplished?

Although the range of premises available to fill in the syllogism may seem extremely wide, the actual set of choices is significantly constrained by a variety of factors. The most important constraints are:

1. The premises must yield the desired conclusion;
2. All terms of the syllogism must match;
3. The specification of any two terms specifies the third;
4. The premises must be true.

Each of these constraints is discussed below.

§ 3.2. The Premises Must Yield the Desired Conclusion.

The most obvious constraint on the choice of premises, and also the most powerful, is that the premises must yield the desired conclusion. At this point in the construction of your argument, you have already converted your position into the conclusion of your syllogism. Clearly, you must build a syllogism that yields only the conclusion you have determined to be necessary, and no other. If you construct a syllogism that yields a conclusion that does not support your position, *you will lose.*

§ 3.3. All Terms Must Match.

Another feature of syllogistic argument that narrows the universe of potentially useful premises is the requirement that all terms of the syllogism match each other exactly. Recall that the persuasiveness of a syllogism derives from its basis in the transitivity principle: if A = B, and B = C, then A = C. This relationship holds only when A, B, and C consistently represent the same variables. For example, the following syllogism does not work:

1. All men are mortal.
2. Socrates is a dog.
3. Therefore, Socrates is mortal.

It is possible that the premises and conclusion of this syllogism are all true. Nevertheless, the syllogism itself is incorrect as a statement of logical relation, and is therefore unpersuasive, because it violates the transitivity principle. To see this, assign the variables A to Socrates, B to men, C to mortals, and D to dog.

1. All men are mortal. [B = C]
2. Socrates is a dog. [A = D]
3. Therefore, Socrates is mortal. [A = C]

The syllogism fails the transitivity principle because it leaps from one proposition (B = C) to a completely unrelated one (A = D) – the major premise bears no connection to the minor premise.

The transitivity principle is a demanding taskmaster. It requires that the terms of the premises and conclusion match *exactly*. Even the slightest deviation among terms is sufficient to rob the syllogism of its persuasive power. Consider the following syllogism, the terms of which match each other more closely than in the previous example:

1. All men are mortal.
2. Socrates appears to be a man.
3. Therefore, Socrates is mortal.

This syllogism suffers from exactly the same defect as the previous one: the terms of the major and minor premises do not match *exactly,* and the syllogism therefore violates the transitivity principle. In order for transitivity to hold, one of the premises must be recast. For example, we could recast the major premise as follows:

1. Things that appear to be men are mortal.
2. Socrates appears to be a man.
3. Therefore, Socrates is mortal.

This form maintains the exact identity of variables from the major to the minor premise, and the syllogism now correctly states a logical relationship.

It is especially easy to violate the transitivity principle in legal argument because legal terms and propositions are often vague. Suppose you are challenging a law on equal protection grounds as racially discriminatory. You find in your research that the Constitution permits the government to pass a law that classifies people according to race only if the law serves a "compelling government interest." Consider the following syllogism:

1. A law that classifies people by race is constitutional only if it serves a compelling government interest.
2. This law classifying people by race does not serve any important government interest.
3. Therefore, this law is unconstitutional.

This syllogism violates the transitivity principle: the major premise refers to "compelling" government interests, but the minor premise refers to "important" government interests. Because the transitivity principle demands complete identity between terms, the minor premise should be:

2. This law does not serve a *compelling* government interest.

Now, you may be skeptical about the legal difference between a government interest that is "important" and one that is "compelling." You may feel that both terms are so imprecise that no meaningful distinction exists between them, and that they therefore may be used interchangeably. Resist this feeling; it is an inadequate justification for departing from the strict requirements of transitivity. If there *is* a legal difference between "important" and "compelling," then your syllogism fails and will be unpersuasive. If there is *no* legal difference between the two terms, you will still have to explain that fact to the court in order to justify your indiscriminate use of two different terms. This will needlessly complicate your argument, and any needless complication should be avoided. Consequently, the strict requirements of transitivity should always be scrupulously observed.

§ 3.4. The Specification of Any Two Terms Specifies the Third.

The internal logic of syllogisms also constrains the selection of premises in another way. Because syllogisms rely on the transitivity principle, specifying any two terms of the syllogism automatically specifies the third term.

We already know that the conclusion follows automatically from the major and minor premises. But we can also deduce the minor premise if we know the major premise and the conclusion, and we can deduce the major premise if we know the minor premise and the conclusion. That is, if we know one premise (A = B), and the conclusion (A = C), then we can specify the other premise (B = C).

For example, suppose we know from analyzing our position that our conclusion must be: "Therefore, the court has diversity jurisdiction over plaintiff's claim." Suppose further that we know our major premise is: "A federal court has diversity jurisdiction only over claims exceeding $50,000." This gives us three variables: (A) a federal court's diversity jurisdiction, (B) claims exceeding $50,000, and (C) plaintiff's claim. Here is what we have so far:

1. A federal court has diversity jurisdiction only over claims exceeding $50,000. [A = B]
2.
3. Therefore, a federal court has diversity jurisdiction over plaintiff's claim. [A = C]

It is clear that this syllogism will be complete only if the minor premise establishes the equivalence of plaintiff's claim and claims exceeding $50,000 – that is, the minor premise must establish that B = C (or C = B, which is the same thing). Therefore, the minor premise *must* be:

2. Plaintiff's claim exceeds $50,000. [C = B]

Note that we can deduce what the minor premise must be without actually knowing if the premise is true.

The same process can be used to determine the major premise if the conclusion and minor premise are known. Suppose we have:

1.
2. Plaintiff's claim exceeds $50,000.
3. Therefore, a federal court has diversity jurisdiction over plaintiff's claim.

From this we can deduce that the major premise must be:

1. A federal court has diversity jurisdiction over claims exceeding $50,000.

§ 3.5. The Premises Must Be True.

The final constraint on the selection of premises for a syllogism is the simplest: the premise must be true. Unlike the other constraints we have examined, this one arises not from the internal logic of the syllogism itself, but from external circumstances – namely, the fact that the syllogism will be used to mount an argument intended to persuade another person.

There will almost always be more than one set of premises that yields any desired conclusion, and often there will be many. For example, suppose we know that the conclusion to our syllogism is: "Therefore, Socrates is mortal." We know at least one set of premises that yields this conclusion:

1. All men are mortal.
2. Socrates is a man.
3. Therefore, Socrates is mortal.

But this is hardly the only set of premises that yields the desired conclusion. Here are two others that will do as well.

1. All parrots are mortal.
2. Socrates is a parrot.
3. Therefore, Socrates is mortal.

1. Someone who can never die is mortal.
2. Socrates can never die.
3. Therefore, Socrates is mortal.

Both of these syllogisms are internally consistent, and both yield the required conclusion. That does not mean, however, that we must accept and use them in an argument. We may reject the first syllogism because its minor premise is false: Socrates is a man, not a parrot. Similarly, the major premise of the second syllogism defines "mortal" incorrectly. Thus, constraints on the acceptability of premises arise not from the internal logic of the syllogism itself, but from what we know to be true about the subject matter of the syllogism. That is, premises must be judged not only by whether they yield the desired conclusion, but also by their accuracy.

§ 3.6. A Recursive Process.

Unfortunately, there is no strictly mechanical way to generate the premises of a syllogism to which the conclusion is known. As a result, the process of filling in the premises of a syllogistic argument is necessarily a *recursive,* or trial-and-error process. That is, we choose one premise as a provisional starting point. Since our conclusion is known in advance, the choice of one premise necessarily determines the other. We then evaluate that premise. Is it true? Does it lead logically to the proper conclusion? If not then we must adjust it. But any adjustment to the second premise requires a corresponding adjustment to the first. We make that adjustment and then evaluate the reformed first premise. If necessary, we readjust it, continuing in a like manner until we have a syllogism with two satisfactory premises that yield precisely the desired conclusion.

Here is an example of the type of recursive reasoning process used in the determination of the premises of a syllogistic legal argument. Suppose our client is a doctor who is a member of a medical practice group. She comes to us with the following problem. She is no longer happy in her group practice, and wishes to leave the group in order to establish her own practice. However, her contract with the group contains a "no-compete" clause. The clause says that if she leaves the group, she agrees not to establish her own practice within a ten-mile radius of the group's location for a period of five years. She now finds this restriction unacceptable. The ten-mile limit would push her entirely out of the city in which she has lived and worked all her career and where the majority of her potential clients are, and she cannot wait five years to establish a practice within the city. She wants to know if there is any way she can get out of complying with the no-compete clause.

After some preliminary research, we find that in our jurisdiction the courts consider a no-compete clause limitation to be enforceable only if it is "reasonable." If it is "unreasonable," the courts will not enforce it. Since we know from our alignment in this conflict that we want the courts *not* to enforce the clause, it follows that our position must be: this no-compete limitation is unreasonable. Converting this position to a syllogism, we have so far:

1.
2.
3. Therefore, this no-compete limitation is unreasonable.

Suppose we now look more closely at the case law. We find that the leading decision in our jurisdiction involved an accountant who violated a clause setting a noncompetition radius of twelve miles. The court held that this restriction was unreasonable. Let us say provisionally that this case allows us to formulate the following proposition of law: a no-compete limitation of twelve miles or more is unreasonable. Suppose we try this out as our major premise:

1. A no-compete limitation of twelve miles or more is unreasonable.
2.
3. Therefore, this no-compete limitation is unreasonable.

Since we now have one premise and the conclusion, we can mechanically fill in the other premise. In order for the syllogism to stand as a logical statement, it must now read:

1. A no-compete limitation of twelve miles or more is unreasonable.
2. This no-compete limitation is twelve miles or more.
3. Therefore, this no-compete limitation is unreasonable.

This syllogism states a winning legal argument. Unfortunately, though, we can't use this syllogism; the minor premise is false. The no-compete clause here specifies a limit of *ten* miles, not twelve. We need to win in this case, not some other case with different facts. Let's substitute the minor premise we know to be true:

1. A no-compete limitation of twelve miles or more is unreasonable.
2. This no-compete limitation is *ten* miles or more.
3. Therefore, this no-compete limitation is unreasonable.

But now we have a different problem: the terms of the syllogism no longer match and it proves nothing. In order to reconstruct the syllogism to state a logical relationship, we must revise our provisional major premise:

1. A no-compete limitation of *ten* miles or more is unreasonable.
2. This no-compete limitation is ten miles or more.
3. Therefore, this no-compete limitation is unreasonable.

Once again we have a winning, properly formed syllogism. Better yet, the minor premise is true. The only question now is whether the major premise is also true. Is it a correct statement of law? We know this much: it had better be a correct statement of law or we need to go back to the drawing board.

It would be best, of course, to find a case that said exactly what we want the major premise of our syllogism to say. Here, though, the case law appears to provide no definitive answer. That's not so bad; perhaps we can come up with some plausible argument in support of the major premise.

For example, we might be able to argue that a twelve-mile limit for accountants is equivalent to a ten-mile limit for doctors because the services of accountants are less in demand than those of doctors.

If, on the other hand, further research and reflection convinces us that there is no good argument in support of the major premise, we may have to substitute a different major premise, requiring a further revision of the minor premise. For example, if the distance aspect of the limitation proves unhelpful, we might try focusing on the duration of the restriction, or on the specific combination of distance and duration. Thus, instead of framing the legal principle as "ten-mile limitations are unreasonable," we might substitute "five-year restrictions are unreasonable," or "ten-mile, five-year restrictions are unreasonable." Whatever the outcome, this type of back and forth movement from premise to premise within a framework provided by a fixed conclusion is the essence of the recursive process of premise determination.

§ 3.7. The Indeterminacy of Law.

The analysis of the previous section may prove surprising to some. We saw there that both premises of a syllogism may need to be tinkered with and adjusted in order to yield the desired conclusion. But we said earlier that the major premise of a legal syllogism states a proposition of law. How can a legal proposition be "adjusted" to yield a specified result? The law is externally fixed by courts and legislatures, so doesn't it follow that a statement of the law is either correct or not? And if so, how can an advocate tinker with a legal premise without also making it false?

The truth, perhaps unfortunately, is that there is far more play in the joints of the law than the fiction of legal determinacy would have us believe. In order to be useful for a wide variety of situations, a legal rule must be abstract and general to some degree. This generality inevitably gives rise to some amount of uncertainty in the rule's meaning and application. It is the lawyer's job to exploit any uncertainty by attempting to "fill in" a gray area of the law in a way favorable to the client.

Of course, it is hardly true that *any* argument at all will be acceptable; the general contours of the law usually set some limits on the types of arguments that can be considered contextually plausible. (Some of these limits are discussed further in Chapter 13.) The bottom line is that an advocate's view of the law is dictated primarily by the client's position, and only secondarily by the actual, discernible contours of the doctrinal landscape. This feature of legal practice has greatly contributed to the public impression that lawyers are amoral "hired guns" who will say whatever it takes to win for their clients. But this same feature of legal practice also makes legal advocacy a creative and challenging enterprise.

Chapter 4

GROUNDING THE PREMISES

§ 4.1. The Requirement of Grounding.
§ 4.2. Directly Grounded Premises.
§ 4.3. Indirect Grounding Through Nested Syllogisms.
§ 4.4. Multiple Grounding.
§ 4.5. Grounding in Controversial First Principles.

§ 4.1. The Requirement of Grounding.

Each syllogism is its own little world; it is an internally coherent view of a certain limited universe. But a syllogism's internal consistency provides no guarantee that any particular person will accept its argument; one can admit a syllogism's logic and still reject its conclusion because one rejects its premises. A critical task for any advocate, then, is to induce his or her target audience to accept the premises of a syllogistic argument.

What induces someone to accept the premise of a syllogism? At a minimum, the targets of persuasion must believe the premise of a syllogism to be true before they will accept it as the basis for a persuasive argument. That is why, as we saw in Chapter 3, the advocate must offer only premises that are true.

But is the truth of a syllogism enough to persuade an audience to accept it? Consider the following syllogism:

1. Airfoils generate lift according to Bernoulli's Principle.
2. A fixed aircraft wing is an airfoil.
3. Therefore, a fixed aircraft wing generates lift according to Bernoulli's Principle.

This syllogism states a true explanation of why an airplane flies. It is properly structured and internally coherent. But does it persuade you? Probably not, unless you happen to know something about fluid mechanics.

The premise of a syllogism, then, must be something more than merely true; it must be *grounded*. To say that a premise is grounded means that the premise is not only true, but *self-evidently* true; it requires no further explanation or justification from the advocate. A grounded premise is one that the target audience will accept as true without further elaboration.

Now reconsider the foregoing syllogism explaining why airplanes fly. Since most people lack sufficient information to discern the truth of this syllogism, the syllogism does not persuade them. Most of us need to know the meaning of the terms "airfoil," "Bernoulli's Principle," and "fixed aircraft wing." We need to know why airfoils work according to Bernoulli's Principle, and why a fixed aircraft wing should be considered an airfoil. Only when we have this information do we have a realistic opportunity to make a judgment about the truth of the premises of this syllogism.

Does this mean that the syllogism is ungrounded? Not necessarily. The syllogism might be sufficiently grounded for presentation at an aeronautical engineering convention; that is, engineers might accept the premises as true without requiring further explanation or justification. But the premises are certainly not sufficiently grounded to present to a jury in a tort suit arising out of a plane crash: a panel of lay persons will require far more explanation than the premises of the syllogism provide.

Proper grounding, then, is a matter of context. The proponent of a syllogism must provide sufficient explanation of its premises to allow the particular target audience to understand why the premises are true.

§ 4.2. Directly Grounded Premises.

There are two types of grounded premises. A *directly grounded* premise is one that is itself properly grounded; the premise states a true proposition that either cannot or need not be further explained. An *indirectly grounded* premise, in contrast, is one that is shown to be true only by linking it to some other premise, which is itself directly or indirectly grounded.

When is a premise directly grounded? Some premises may be incapable of further explanation in virtually any circumstances. For example, it is hard to imagine how one could further ground the proposition "apples are red." Redness is a quality by which we define apples, and it seems impossible to "explain" the word "red." Or consider the statement "all men are mortal." We could probably ground this statement further by explaining the concepts of "man" and "mortality," and we might do so to a small child. But when we are addressing adults, these additional explanations are unnecessary, so the proposition is directly grounded for most purposes.

The premise "the Chief Justice is the head of the judicial branch" is directly grounded for purposes of making an argument in a legal context because every judge and lawyer knows it to be true (or had better know it!). However, the same premise might be ungrounded when directed to an elementary school class, or to a foreigner who lacks a working understanding of the structure of the United States government.

Other examples of premises that would be considered directly grounded in many circumstances might include:

> George Washington was the first President of the United States.
>
> The sun never shines at night.

France is a European country.

Driving without wearing a seatbelt is dangerous.

People should eat healthful and nutritious meals.

§ 4.3. Indirect Grounding Through Nested Syllogisms.

Advocacy would be much simpler if all premises were directly grounded – if the judge could look at the advocate's premises and understand them to be true at a glance. Unfortunately, it is often the case that advocates must construct syllogistic arguments using premises that are not self-evidently true, and which require further explanation in order to gain acceptance. All premises must be grounded. But if a premise is not directly grounded how can its truth be demonstrated? Such premises must be grounded *indirectly*.

Indirect grounding involves taking an ungrounded premise and linking it, through other syllogisms, to a directly grounded premise. Indirect grounding is a four-step process:

1. Identify the ungrounded premise.
2. Convert the ungrounded premise to the conclusion of a new syllogism.
3. Construct new premises for the new syllogism leading to the required conclusion.
4. Evaluate the new premises to see if they are directly grounded. If they are directly grounded, stop. If not, repeat the process until all premises are directly grounded.

This procedure of indirect grounding results in a set of "nested" syllogisms that link the ultimate syllogism indirectly to a set of premises that are directly grounded and thus require no further justification.

Here is an example of indirect grounding. Suppose you wish to persuade your local town council to install a traffic light at a dangerous intersection near your house, and you present the following argument:

1. Traffic lights should be installed at dangerous intersections.
2. The intersection of North Street and Main Street is dangerous.
3. Therefore, a traffic light should be installed at the intersection of North and Main.

Now suppose that you judge the major premise to be adequately grounded as far as the town council is concerned; you think the council members will accept the major premise as self-evidently true. The minor premise, however, may present problems. Let's assume that it is not directly grounded.

In order to ground the minor premise indirectly according to the method set out above, you must first convert the premise into the conclusion of a new syllogism:

1.
2.
3. Therefore, the intersection of North and Main is dangerous.

The next step is to fill in the premises of this new syllogism. Note that performing this step forces you to analyze your own implicit assumptions and premises. Why *do* you think that this intersection is a dangerous one?

Let's assume that you think the intersection is dangerous because there have been many accidents there – say, one a month. That information might give us the following syllogism:

1. An intersection is dangerous if it is the site of one or more accidents per month.
2. The intersection of North and Main is the site of at least one accident per month.
3. Therefore, the intersection of North and Main is dangerous.

The final step is to see if the premises of the new syllogism are directly grounded. Are they? As we have seen, the answer to this question depends on the context. Perhaps most town councils would accept the major premise of this syllogism without further argument. If you think your council would, you may consider the major premise directly grounded. On the other hand, it is possible to imagine a town council requiring further explanation for the major premise. For example, the council might respond: "Dangerous compared to what? Maybe an accident rate of one per month makes the intersection a relatively safe one in comparison to other intersections in the town."

If you really wanted to be sure of making your case persuasively, you might decide to treat the major premise of the new syllogism as requiring further grounding. You would again need to examine your own assumptions and premises: why *do* you think that an accident rate of one per month makes an intersection dangerous? Perhaps you might come up with a new syllogism along the following lines:

1. An intersection is dangerous if its monthly accident rate exceeds the average monthly accident rate for all intersections in the town.
2. The average monthly accident rate for all intersections in the town is just under one accident per month.
3. Therefore, an intersection is dangerous if it is the site of one or more accidents per month.

As before, you would then need to ask yourself whether each of these premises is adequately grounded, and so on. Eventually, though, you will come to a point beyond which further explanation is impossible or unnecessary. When such a point is reached, your original syllogism is indirectly grounded.

The following diagram summarizes the indirect grounding process set out above.

1. Traffic lights should be installed at dangerous intersections.
2. The intersection of North Street and Main Street is dangerous.
3. Therefore, a traffic light should be installed at the intersection of North and Main.

1. An intersection is dangerous if it is the site of one or more accidents per month.
2. The intersection of North and Main is the site of at least one accident per month.
3. Therefore, the intersection of North and Main is dangerous.

1. An intersection is dangerous if its monthly accident rate exceeds the average monthly accident rate for all intersections in the town.
2. The average monthly accident rate for all intersections in the town is just under one accident per month.
3. Therefore, an intersection is dangerous if it is the site of one or more accidents per month.

§4.4. Multiple Grounding.

In the traffic light example given above, the ungrounded premise was grounded through a single series of nested syllogisms. This set of nested syllogisms defined a single, straight-line path from the premise to its ground. It is often the case, however, that an ungrounded premise can be supported in more than one way, and that it can therefore be grounded at more than one point.

For example, suppose that the intersection of North and Main discussed above is dangerous not only because there is an accident there every month, but because children cross the intersection on their way to school. This could lead to an entirely different set of nested syllogisms grounded in an entirely different premise. Here is one possibility:

1. An intersection is dangerous if children routinely use it on their way to school.
2. Children routinely use the intersection of North and Main on their way to school.
3. Therefore, the intersection of North and Main is dangerous.

Again, the premises of this syllogism may be in need of further grounding. If so, the process would continue until an appropriate grounding point is reached.

Multiple grounding strengthens an argument by increasing the chances that an ungrounded premise will be accepted by the decision maker. If, for some reason, a court rejects one route to ground as unpersuasive, the advocate has not necessarily lost the argument; the court might still accept a different route.

This does not mean, of course, that an advocate should bury a court in as many multiple groundings as he or she can conceive for each and every premise. Not every grounding will be equally persuasive, and where some possible groundings are stronger than others the advocate should use only the stronger ones. Excessive grounding should also be avoided if it will only lead to confusion. Finally, excessive grounding risks weakening the overall presentation by conveying the impression that the advocate has attempted to pile on as many arguments as possible because he or she lacks faith in the persuasive power of the arguments individually.

§ 4.5. Grounding in Controversial First Principles.

Most premises can be grounded in uncontroversial propositions or in verifiable assertions of fact. Some premises, however, can only be grounded in propositions that are sufficiently controversial to make their acceptance problematic for people who do not already agree with them.

Consider the example of euthanasia. Those who oppose euthanasia frequently argue that euthanasia is murder. Suppose they rely on an argument like this:

1. Murder is the wrongful taking of human life.
2. Euthanasia is the wrongful taking of human life.
3. Therefore, euthanasia is murder.

If this argument is intended to persuade a supporter of euthanasia, it obviously must be further grounded. The weak spot is probably the minor premise: most supporters of euthanasia would not be willing to accept the proposition that euthanasia involves the "wrongful" taking of human life.

The difficulty here is in figuring out how to further ground the proposition that euthanasia is wrongful. Most attempts at grounding this proposition seem to lead to premises that would be no more acceptable to supporters of euthanasia than the proposition to be grounded. To give just one example, some opponents of euthanasia argue that life, even when it is painful or hopeless, is preferable to death. Suppose their argument implicitly goes something like this:

1. To make someone worse off is wrong.
2. Euthanasia makes a person worse off.
3. Therefore, euthanasia is wrong.

It is doubtful that this syllogism would provide any better grounding as far as supporters of euthanasia are concerned. Most euthanasia advocates would probably dispute the proposition that death can never make a terminally ill patient better off. It might be possible to go further; one could assert, for instance, that the aches and pains of life are nothing compared to the horrors of death – but it is far from clear how that proposition could be further grounded. Either you believe it or you don't, or so it seems.

At this point, further explanation or justification for this premise appears impossible. This is the aim of the grounding process. Yet despite having properly grounded the premise, we still have not arrived at a bedrock proposition that *must* be accepted.

Unfortunately, there is no way out of this difficulty. Just because a premise cannot be further explained or justified does not mean that everyone must automatically accept it. Every system of thought contains certain first principles, or *axioms,* that cannot be explained within the system; they are propositions that simply must be accepted as true, and on which the rest of the system of thought is built. Grounding a premise can thus explain and justify it only to one who already accepts the axioms on which it is based.

One of the things that makes communication difficult in our world is that different people sometimes hold different and even contradictory axioms, causing them occasionally to move in what may with some justice be called different systems of thought. Moreover, convincing someone to accept a new axiom, particularly if doing so involves his or her rejection of a previously held axiom, is one of life's most difficult tasks. Persuasion on this level more closely resembles a religious conversion than a voluntary and rational decision to accept an argument.

From these observations the advocate can draw two lessons. First, all the advocate can ever do is follow his or her premises to ground, wherever they may lead. The most important task for the advocate here is simply to recognize when a premise is incapable of further explanation or justification and is thus adequately grounded. Beyond this point the advocate cannot go.

Second, when there is a choice, the advocate should attempt to ground premises in those propositions that the judge is most likely to accept. When possible, the advocate should avoid grounding premises in highly controversial, axiomatic principles that the judge may not share. At the very least, the advocate should always try to offer an uncontroversial route to ground as an alternative to a more controversial route. The advocate's goal, after all, is to win the case, not to make a convert of the judge.

PART II

ELEMENTS OF PERSUASIVE LEGAL ARGUMENT

Chapter 5

THE MAJOR PREMISE

§ 5.1. Introduction.
§ 5.2. The Basic Strategy.
§ 5.3. Establishing Certainty of Authoritativeness.
  § 5.3.1. Sources of Authority.
  § 5.3.2. Direct Grounding in Targeted Authority.
  § 5.3.3. Indirect Grounding of the Major Premise.
§ 5.4. Establishing Certainty in Content.
  § 5.4.1. Tests.
  § 5.4.2. Step Analysis.
  § 5.4.3. Factor Analysis.
  § 5.4.4. A Factor Analysis Can Always Be Extracted.
  § 5.4.5. The Utility of Lower Court Decisions.

§ 5.1. Introduction.

In any legal struggle, the real action is in the contest over the premises. Although the court's acceptance or rejection of the parties' conclusions will determine ultimately who wins and who loses, the parties' conclusions, as we have seen, are fixed by their alignments and do not change during the litigation. Thus, the most important variable by far in a legal dispute concerns the characterization of the law and facts. The party that succeeds in getting the court to accept its characterizations of law and fact – its premises – will inevitably prevail.

In the last chapter, we saw that a premise must be grounded if it is to be accepted. We also saw that proper grounding is largely a matter of context: what grounds a premise varies from audience to audience depending upon the beliefs and assumptions of the audience and the purposes for which the argument is advanced. In this chapter and the next we therefore turn directly to the question of how to ground the major and minor premises of a *legal* argument – that is, an argument made by a lawyer to a court in a legal case. What premises can a legal advocate most successfully advance?

§ 5.2. The Basic Strategy.

The most effective way to persuade a judge to accept *your* major premise, *your* characterization of the law, is to create the impression that *the judge has no choice*. The most effective advocate will try to make the judge's job seem so easy, and so mechanical, that the judge must accept the advocate's characterization of the law as correct and agree to its application to the facts of the case. No litigator is more in heaven than when he or she hears the judge say gravely to opposing counsel: "I'm sorry, but I'm afraid I have no choice but to rule against you."

Judges often exercise a good deal of discretion in the resolution of cases. But the need to exercise such discretion often presents the judge with difficult decisions. Judges are human beings, and no human being likes to make hard choices. The advocate can exploit this tendency by convincing the judge that *this* case simply is not one that calls for the exercise of discretion; quite to the contrary, this is a case in which any decisions are so routine and mechanical that the judge can proceed as though on automatic pilot.

How does the advocate create the impression that the judge has no discretion and that the outcome is virtually foreordained? Where the major premise is concerned, the advocate does so by creating an impression of *certainty in the law*. That is, the advocate must create the impression that there can be no doubt whatever about which legal rules apply in this case, nor can there be the slightest doubt about the specific content of those rules.

There are two distinct and equally important aspects to the establishment of the impression of certainty in the law:

certainty of *authoritativeness,* and certainty of *content.* Each of these is discussed below.

§ 5.3. Establishing Certainty of Authoritativeness.

§ 5.3.1. Sources of Authority.

The quickest and most indispensable way to convince a court that it has no choice but to accept a particular view of the law expressed in the major premise of a legal argument is to demonstrate that someone with more authority than the court itself possesses has advanced this view. If someone with more authority than the court has said what the law is, then the court has no business saying otherwise and must obediently comply.

Who has such authority and how is it expressed? In our legal system, there are three main possibilities:

A. A directly supervising court, as expressed in controlling precedent on point.
B. The legislature, as expressed in a statute.
C. The people, as expressed in a constitution.

When one of these entities says what the law is, its statement of the law is authoritative – that statement *is* the law as far as the judge can be concerned.

Although constitutions, statutes, and directly controlling case precedents are the only sources of authority to which they *must* defer, judges often perceive certain non-binding sources of authority to be almost as compelling. For example, there are a few "big guns" whose views are often treated as authoritative: James Madison, Alexander Hamilton, Thomas Jefferson, John Marshall, Oliver Wendell Holmes, and Louis Brandeis usually fit this description. In addition, a judge might accept as authoritative the pronouncements of other sources he or she considers worthy of respect – certain courts or judges from other jurisdictions, for example, or the various Restatements of Law – even if those pronouncements are not technically binding. But none of these non-binding sources of authority is ever as persuasive as the three binding sources mentioned above.

§ 5.3.2. Direct Grounding in Targeted Authority.

The major premise of every legal argument carries with it an implicit representation by the advocate to the court that the law really is what the advocate says it is. To make good on this representation – to ground the premise – the advocate must show a link between the major premise and the pronouncement of an authoritative source of law. That is, the advocate must show that the major premise says nothing other than what some higher authority has already decreed the law to be. A major premise that satisfies this condition will be considered directly grounded by a court. The court will require no further justification; the fact that an authoritative source said it is enough.

One way to see what legal grounding is necessary is to imagine the following dialogue between the advocate and the judge every time the advocate makes a representation concerning the law:

ADVOCATE: Your Honor, here's what the law is: in order for a federal court to have diversity jurisdiction, there must be complete diversity between the parties.

JUDGE: Oh, yeah? Says who?

ADVOCATE: Says the United States Supreme Court in *Strawbridge v. Curtiss*.

JUDGE: Oh. Well, in that case, proceed.

In other words, the court needs reassurance that your statement of the law really *is* the law. Thus, to persuade the court that your argument is correct and must be accepted, you need to do more than merely produce an internally consistent syllogism. You must also ground the major premise by establishing its legal certainty.

How does one go about linking a statement of law contained in a major premise to a targeted authoritative legal source? This subject is the bread and butter of every first year legal writing course, so we can make do here with the briefest summary.

A. *Cite Case Authority*

Where your source of authority is a court, you establish a direct link between your premise and the authority simply by citing the case in which the pertinent language appears. By universal convention, a sentence followed by a citation constitutes a representation that the cited case says in substance just what the preceding sentence says. If the precise language of the court is especially important, or if you have reason to think that the judge may be skeptical of your representations concerning the content of the authority you are relying on, you may reinforce the link by quoting directly from the authoritative case. In general, though, it is sufficient to paraphrase the court's language.

A common misperception among beginning law students is that a case decided by a higher court is useless as authority unless it is factually analogous to the case at hand. This misperception results from a failure to distinguish the court's holding from its statements of the law. Like a legal argument, a judicial opinion consists of a statement of legal principles, an application of those principles to the facts of the case, and a conclusion. The court's opinion can serve as authority for one, two or all three of these aspects of its ruling. The precedential value of the ruling thus depends on the purpose for which it is being cited. Consequently, a court's statements of the law are good authority for what the law is, even if those statements are made in cases factually different from the one at hand. In supporting a major premise, then, it is unnecessary for the advocate to demonstrate any factual analogy between the cited case and the case at hand; it is enough simply to assert the rule of law and cite to the pertinent case:

> In order for a federal court to have diversity jurisdiction, there must be complete diversity between the parties. *Strawbridge v. Curtiss.*

B. *Quote Statutes or Cite Their Interpretations*

If the targeted source of authority is a statute, quote it. Because a statute *is* law in a way that judicial opinions are not, you present the law authoritatively merely by quoting the statutory language. The same is true of other written sources of positive law such as constitutions and regulations.[5]

A straightforward presentation of the statutory language is especially powerful because of the so-called "plain meaning rule." This rule (or "canon") of statutory construction, much maligned by legal academics but relied on daily by judges across the nation, directs courts to interpret

---

[5] There are a few statutes that are so long, cumbersome or complicated that quoting them will cause more confusion than clarification. In those rare cases, it is appropriate to paraphrase the statute, but even then it is best to include an appendix containing the actual statutory language. No judge will decide a statutory case based solely on a lawyer's second-hand representation of what the statute says; the judge will want to see for himself or herself.

statutes according to their plain meaning whenever possible. Thus, the authoritativeness of a major premise based on statutory law can be powerfully established merely by quoting the statute itself and referring the court to the plain meaning rule.

There are many other canons of statutory construction that assist courts in the interpretation of statutes and to which the advocate should remain alert. These canons, which have generally been fashioned by courts and are found in judicial opinions, can often be used as persuasive support for the advocate's reading of the statute.

Another way to demonstrate the correctness of a proffered reading of a statute (or constitution) is to show that a higher court has interpreted the statute in that way. In our system, a higher court's reading of statutory law is as binding on lower courts as if the legislature itself had written the court's reading into the statutory language. Thus, if the Supreme Court has said, for example, that a state judicial election is an "election" within the meaning of the Voting Rights Act, that's the law – that's what the Voting Rights Act means.

C. *Use Multiple Sources of Authority*

The strongest way of all to show the authoritativeness of a major premise is to link it not merely to one authoritative source of law, but to several. No demonstration could be more convincing to a judge than to show that Congress, the Supreme Court of the United States, and the directly supervising appellate court all conceive the law to be precisely what you, the advocate, say it is. Always keep in mind that there is a kind of subtext to your presentation of the major premise that goes something like this: "Don't worry, Judge. I'm going to tell you what the law is, and I'm going to tell it to you straight. You can rely on me, Judge.

I'll help you reach a decision in this case that will faithfully apply the law – and one that won't be reversed on appeal."

§ 5.3.3. Indirect Grounding of the Major Premise.

We have been dealing so far with situations in which the major premise of the legal argument is simply a direct recapitulation of something that an authoritative legal source has already said. For example, suppose that the highest court in our jurisdiction said in *Garrison v. Hughes,* "in order to be enforceable, a contract must be supported by consideration"; and suppose that we want to use this proposition as the major premise of a legal argument. All we have said so far is that the major premise should be linked to the ruling of the high court by a direct citation:

1. In order to be enforceable, a contract must be supported by consideration. *Garrison v. Hughes.*

The use of the citation directly grounds the premise in the targeted source of legal authority.

But what if the major premise that we wish to use has *not* been specifically proclaimed in so many words by an authoritative legal source? If it is to persuade a court, the major premise must still be grounded in some authoritative legal pronouncement. If the premise cannot be grounded directly, however, the only alternative is to ground it indirectly.

A legal premise is indirectly grounded in the same way as any other premise (see Chapter 4). The ungrounded major premise of the argument is converted into the conclusion of a new syllogism, the premises of which are then constructed. The major premise of the new syllogism should be a directly grounded statement of the law. If it is not, the process must be repeated until ground is reached.

Here is an example of an indirectly grounded major premise. Suppose we represent the defendant in a contract dispute. The client wants a jury trial, but state law provides that contract cases are to be tried before a judge. We want to argue that the state's refusal to provide a jury trial violates our client's constitutional rights under the seventh amendment. Our goal, then, is to ground the following major premise:

1. The seventh amendment guarantees a jury trial in contract cases.

After performing some research, we find that neither the United States Supreme Court nor any court in our state has ever made such a holding. The premise therefore cannot be directly grounded.

To ground the premise indirectly, we must first convert it to the conclusion of a new syllogism:

1.
2.
3. Therefore, the seventh amendment guarantees a jury trial in contract cases.

Now suppose we find in our research that the Supreme Court said in *Curtis v. Loether* that the seventh amendment guarantees a jury trial in those types of civil cases for which a jury trial was available in 1791 (the date of the amendment's ratification). This is a premise that can be directly grounded. Let's try it as the major premise of the new syllogism:

1. The seventh amendment guarantees a jury trial in those types of civil cases for which a jury trial was available in 1791. *Curtis v. Loether.*

2.
3. Therefore, the seventh amendment guarantees a jury trial in contract cases.

Since we now have two terms of the syllogism, we can fill in the remaining term mechanically:

1. The seventh amendment guarantees a jury trial in those types of civil cases for which a jury trial was available in 1791. *Curtis v. Loether.*
2. A jury trial was available in 1791 in contract cases.
3. Therefore, the seventh amendment guarantees a jury trial in contract cases.

As a matter of law, then, this syllogism is directly grounded, and the major premise of the original syllogism is indirectly grounded, which was our goal. Of course, our work is far from done: the minor premise of the new syllogism contains an assertion of historical fact that must also be grounded. A discussion of the grounding of minor premises is deferred until Chapter 6.

The preceding example illustrates one additional good practice in the indirect grounding of legal premises: it is usually best to ground legal premises ultimately in something that a court or legislature has actually and literally said. Sometimes advocates will try to ground legal premises in, for example, "implicit" judicial holdings. In such arguments the advocate claims, in essence: "The court may not have said proposition X in so many words, but proposition X is implicit in the court's ruling."

An argument based on an implicit holding may appear to ground a legal premise, but this appearance can sometimes be illusory. In a sense, an implicit holding is by definition ungrounded: what makes a holding implicit rather than explicit is that there is some unstated syllogism lurking in the background that links the court's explicit language to the implicit holding. Consequently, it is usually best to lay bare the unstated syllogism underlying the assertion that the argument is implicit, thereby grounding the argument in the court's actual words – a much more tangible and readily grasped grounding point. At the very least, any time you do want to treat as directly grounded a legal premise based on an implicit holding, you must be very sure that the implicit holding is so obvious that the judge is sure to see it.

§ 5.4. Establishing Certainty in Content.

The second, equally important task necessary to create the requisite impression of legal certainty is the establishment of certainty in the *content* of the law. Establishing certainty of authoritativeness creates the impression that the court has received instructions from an authoritative source, but this is not enough. The advocate must also make the instructions themselves seem as clear and precise as possible.

The law is often vague. What then can the advocate do to create the impression that the content of the applicable law is clear and certain? The key is to formulate your major premise, whenever possible, using the *language of tests, steps, or factors*. A legal premise formulated in any one of these ways carries with it an air of precision and authority that simply cannot be attained in any other way. Moreover, the presentation of the law in the form of a prepackaged test, step, or factor analysis makes the court's task of applying the law seem utterly mechanical – exactly the impression the advocate strives to achieve.

§ 5.4.1. Tests.

A *test* is a formulation of the law expressed as a set of discrete conditions. When the conditions of a test are satisfied or are not – when the test is passed or failed – somebody wins and somebody loses. This is what makes a test seem clear and certain, and its outcome a question of mechanical application.

In case law, a test is easiest to identify when the court specifically identifies it for you. Occasionally, a court will actually say something like: "The test we use here is. . . ." Sometimes a court will number the prongs of the test it has articulated to draw further attention to the test. For example, in *Heart of Atlanta Motel v. United States,* a case involving the constitutionality of a federal civil rights law prohibiting racial discrimination by motels, the Supreme Court said:

> The only questions are: (1) whether Congress had a rational basis for finding that racial discrimination by motels affected commerce, and (2) if it had such a basis, whether the means it selected to eliminate that evil are reasonable and appropriate.

This language establishes a two-prong test for assessing the constitutionality of legislation enacted under the Commerce Clause of the United States Constitution. Note how certain and sure the Court's use of a test makes the analysis appear. According to the Court, there are "only" two questions that need to be addressed. If the Supreme Court has said that only two questions are relevant to a decision on this issue, certainly a lower court can have no business addressing anything else.

Using a test as the major premise of a legal argument is no different from using any other legal proposition:

1. An anti-discrimination law enacted under the Commerce Clause is constitutional if: (1) Congress had a rational basis for finding that the proscribed

> racial discrimination affected commerce, and (2) the means it selected to eliminate that evil are reasonable and appropriate. *Heart of Atlanta Motel v. United States*.

Naturally, a plaintiff in a case to which the test applies must take the position that the challenged law fails the test, and a defendant must argue that the law passes the test.

Sometimes courts establish tests without drawing quite the same amount of attention to their formulation. For instance, in *Allen v. Wright* the Supreme Court set out the following test to determine when a plaintiff has "standing" to sue in federal court under Article III of the Constitution:

> The requirement of standing . . . has a core component derived directly from the Constitution. A plaintiff must allege personal injury fairly traceable to the defendant's allegedly unlawful conduct and likely to be redressed by the requested relief.

The second sentence of this passage can be rearranged to state a three-prong test:

> In order to satisfy the constitutional requirements for standing, a plaintiff must allege:
>
> (1) personal injury
> (2) fairly traceable to the defendant's allegedly unlawful conduct and
> (3) likely to be redressed by the requested relief.

Because tests can be stated unobtrusively in this way, the advocate should always be on the lookout for them, or for language that the advocate plausibly can argue was intended by the court to state an authoritative test.

Like cases, statutes can also provide the advocate with tests. Because statutes are often written with many subsections, the tests sometimes virtually jump off the page. For example, 5 U.S.C. § 552(b)(1), a section of the Freedom of Information Act, provides that the federal government need not disclose information in its possession which is:

> (A) specifically authorized under criteria established by an Executive Order to be kept secret in the interest of national defense or foreign policy and (B) [is] in fact properly classified pursuant to such Executive Order . . . .

This provision thus states a two-part test for deciding when public requests for the disclosure of classified information can be denied.

Once again, like any statutory language, this test can be converted directly into the major premise of a legal argument. The example below sets out the full syllogism.

1. The government need not disclose information that is (A) specifically authorized under criteria established by an Executive Order to be kept secret in the interest of national defense or foreign policy and (B) [is] in fact properly classified pursuant to such Executive Order. 5 U.S.C. § 552(b)(1).
2. The information sought in this case is both specifically authorized under criteria established by an Executive Order to be kept secret in the interest of national defense or foreign policy, and is in fact properly classified pursuant to such Executive Order.
3. Therefore, the government need not disclose the information sought in this case.

§ 5.4.2. Step Analysis.

Closely related to the test, and just as useful for creating an impression of certainty in the law, is the *step analysis*. In a step analysis, a court or statute provides a methodology of legal analysis by setting out authoritatively a definite series of analytic steps that a court must take in order to reach the correct result. In other words, the court or statute says: first, do this; next, do this; finally, do this.

An example of step analysis appears in the Supreme Court's decision in *Chevron v. Natural Resources Defense Council*. The case deals with the question of the degree of respect that a court should afford to a government agency's interpretation of a federal statute. The Court held that federal courts should pursue a two-step inquiry:

> When a court reviews an agency's construction of the statute which it administers, it is confronted with two questions. First, always, is the question whether Congress has directly spoken to the precise question at issue. If the intent of Congress is clear, that is the end of the matter. . . . If, however, the court determines Congress has not directly addressed the precise question at issue, . . . the question for the court is whether the agency's answer is based on a permissible construction of the statute.

Here, the Court has instructed lower courts first to determine whether Congress has "spoken directly" to the issue at hand. If the answer is affirmative, the court should stop. If the answer is negative, the court should go on to step two. Step two requires the court to determine whether the agency's interpretation is "permissible." The step analysis thus provides lower courts with a formula that they can follow mechanically, thereby enhancing the impression of legal certainty that the advocate wishes to convey.

§ 5.4.3. Factor Analysis.

Courts and legislatures generally use a *factor analysis* when they want to maintain a degree of flexibility in the law that a firm test or step analysis might not provide. In a factor analysis, the court or legislature lists a series of factors that are deemed relevant to the outcome of a case without specifying precisely how the factors fit together.

For example, *Thornburg v. Gingles* required the Supreme Court to decide when a state or local election scheme has violated the federal Voting Rights Act, which forbids discrimination against minorities in voting. In the following passage, the Court identified seven factors that might be relevant to an assessment of whether a particular state or locality has violated the Act:

> In order to answer this question, a court must assess ... "objective factors." [The] factors which typically may be relevant [include]: the history of voting-related discrimination in the State . . . ; the extent to which voting in the elections of the State . . . is racially polarized; the extent to which the State . . . has used voting practices or procedures that tend to enhance the opportunity for discrimination . . . ; the exclusion of members of the minority group from candidate slating processes; the extent to which minority group members bear the effects of past discrimination . . . which hinder their ability to participate effectively in the political process; the use of overt or subtle racial appeals in political campaigns; and the extent to which members of the minority group have been elected to public office in the jurisdiction.

Unlike a test or step analysis, an enumeration of relevant factors does not specify how any particular case will come out. Thus, it is not necessary for a plaintiff in a voting rights case to show the existence of all seven of the *Gingles* factors; if the plaintiff had to do that then the Court's language would be a test, not a list of factors. Rather, all a plaintiff can do is attempt to show the existence of as many factors as possible, while the defendant must try to show the absence of as many factors as possible.

§ 5.4.4. A Factor Analysis Can Always Be Extracted.

Suppose you want to rely on a case that contains neither a test, a step analysis, nor a list of factors. What then? Before going on, you might consider choosing a different case. Any case that contains none of these methods of analysis is probably one that is badly written and therefore unlikely to persuade the court before which you are appearing. At the very least, you have chosen an ambiguous case, one that may give your opponent the opportunity to mount a strong argument for an alternative reading.

But suppose nonetheless that you decide the case is one you really must use. Even if no amount of searching turns up language that you can plausibly argue states a test or step analysis, you can almost always extract a factor analysis from a judicial opinion. A judicial opinion can never be about nothing (or so the legal system must hope). In order to decide a case, a court has to examine *something* – it has to turn its attention to some features of the case and discuss them in some way or other.

The things a court discusses in its opinion, whatever they might be, are by definition the aspects of the case that the court thinks important. It follows that you can always generate some sort of factor analysis simply by listing the things that the court chose to discuss. You present such a factor analysis to the court in your own case along these lines: "Although the court in *Howell v. Ingmar* did not say explicitly what analysis it used, the court found the following three aspects of the case important enough to discuss at length: A, B and C. Here, factors A, B and C are all present. . . ."

§ 5.4.5. The Utility of Lower Court Decisions.

The United States Supreme Court and the highest courts of the states decide comparatively few cases each year, and the number of decisions they issue in any given area of law is quite small. This means that these courts are able to give relatively little guidance to the lower courts in any single field of law. Knowing this, high courts sometimes try to make very general pronouncements in order to maximize the guidance they provide.

Lower courts, in contrast, hear many more cases and are less concerned with providing broad guidance on an abstract level. Moreover, lower courts must interpret and apply the high courts' broad pronouncements in all the various settings in which those pronouncements might apply. Lower courts are consequently forced to take a more businesslike approach to adjudication than the state and federal supreme courts. One businesslike tactic is to develop as many concrete tests and step analyses as possible in order to standardize and speed up judicial decision making.

As a result, the opinions of lower courts – for example, the federal Circuit Courts of Appeals – are more likely than high court opinions to contain specific, focused tests and step analyses. Thus, although high court opinions may carry more authority, lower court decisions are often a better source for the specific tests that the advocate needs to create the critical impression of certainty in the law's content.

Chapter 6

THE MINOR PREMISE

§ 6.1. Introduction.
§ 6.2. Establishing Certainty of Authoritativeness.
§ 6.2.1. Ground Factual Assertions in Evidence.
§ 6.2.2. Types of Evidence.
§ 6.2.3. Appeals to Common Sense.
§ 6.3. Establish Certainty of Content By Using Brute Facts.
§ 6.3.1. Brute Facts and Compound Facts.
§ 6.3.2. Break Down Compound Facts Into Brute Facts.
§ 6.4. Elaborate Key Legal Terms.
§ 6.4.1. Legal Aspects of the Minor Premise.
§ 6.4.2. Identify the Key Terms.
§ 6.4.3. Tell the Judge: "Here's How You Know It When You See It."
§ 6.5. Conclusory Argument.
§ 6.6. A Grounded Minor Premise Guides Factual Development.

§ 6.1. Introduction.

We turn now to the final task in the construction of a syllogistic legal argument: applying the law to the facts of the case in a persuasive minor premise. The basic strategy for constructing a persuasive minor premise is the same as for major premises: the advocate should strive to create an impression of certainty. As with major premises, such an impression is created by establishing an impression of certainty in both the authoritativeness and content of the minor premise.

Two differences between major and minor premises make this task more difficult for a minor premise. First, a minor premise almost always deals with facts. Courts are bound to follow the law faithfully, but they are often free to determine the facts; there are thus relatively few instances in which a court must obediently accept a fact on someone else's authority. As a result, it is not always possible to persuade a court that it has no choice but to accept the facts set forth in the minor premise of a legal argument.

Second, the minor premise of a legal argument is usually not a pure assertion of fact but a combination of law and fact. This complicates the grounding of the minor premise because the advocate must sort out the legal from the factual strands and ground them separately.

Despite these difficulties, the advocate can generally create a strong impression of certainty in a minor premise by grounding it in evidence, and by elaborating the meaning of key legal terms.

§ 6.2. Establishing Certainty of Authoritativeness.

§ 6.2.1. Ground Factual Assertions in Evidence.

Because the minor premise of a legal syllogism applies a legal principle to the facts of the case, the minor premise inevitably includes some sort of factual assertion. Like any proposition appearing in the premise of an argument, factual assertions must be grounded if they are to persuade a court.

We saw in the last chapter that the advocate can make a legal premise seem certain by grounding it in some kind of authority. Similarly, where the proposition to be grounded is factual, the advocate creates an impression of certainty in authoritativeness by grounding the factual proposition in *evidence*.

Consider once again our old standby syllogism:

1. All men are mortal.
2. Socrates is a man.
3. Therefore, Socrates is mortal.

Suppose you want to persuade a court to accept the minor premise. This premise consists of an assertion of fact. The judge, however, has no way of knowing whether it is true. Assume that the judge doesn't know Socrates, and hasn't seen Socrates in open court. The judge has only your bare assertion, and you are an advocate, someone with little credibility in such matters. You must therefore ground the minor premise in some form of evidence.

You might, for example, obtain an affidavit from Socrates in which he states under oath that he is a man. The directly grounded minor premise might then be:

2. Socrates is a man. Affidavit of Socrates, ¶ 2.

For additional persuasion you might bring in an expert – perhaps a doctor might perform a physical examination:

2. Socrates is a man. Affidavit of Hippocrates, M.D., ¶ 5.

Note how grounding these premises in evidence lends them an air of authoritativeness that they lack when they are supported by nothing more than the advocate's earnest representation.

Note also that these premises are directly grounded by citation to the evidence. Like citation to legal authority, citation to evidence constitutes a representation by the advocate that the cited source says in substance what the advocate has said in the immediately preceding text. Other examples of directly grounded factual premises might include:

> Center Street crosses Route 11 just south of the entrance to the High School parking lot. Exhibit 6.
>
> The defendant said: "I accept your offer." Affidavit of Melissa L. Carpenter, ¶ 7.
>
> The plaintiff is incorporated in Delaware. Complaint, ¶ 2.

Ms. Willis conceded that she had never met Mr. Hoffman before March 2, 1988. Trial Transcript, page 30, line 16.

Of course, the factual assertions of a minor premise can also be grounded indirectly using the same method as we used to ground legal premises indirectly (§ 5.3.3). Suppose, for example, that our client was injured in an automobile crash when he was unable to stop his car. He is suing the automobile manufacturer because his brakes failed, causing the accident.

Suppose that the factual proposition we wish to ground is "plaintiff's brakes failed," but we have no directly supporting evidence. One way to ground this proposition indirectly might be to create a new syllogism grounded directly in a combination of evidence from the plaintiff and an expert, such as a mechanic:

1. A driver has experienced brake failure when he or she steps on the brake pedal and the pedal sinks to the floor without slowing the car. Affidavit of Joe Mechanic, ¶ 4.
2. When the plaintiff stepped on the brake pedal, the pedal sank to the floor without slowing the car. Affidavit of Plaintiff Ronald Simpson, ¶ 7.
3. Therefore, plaintiff experienced brake failure.

As with any premise, the authoritativeness of factual assertions can be enhanced through multiple grounding (§ 4.4). If a factual assertion can be supported by several different types of evidence, the advocate should not hesitate to construct as many grounding syllogisms as necessary to make use of the supporting evidence. Multiple evidentiary grounding strengthens the premise by increasing the chances that a court will accept it as true. Even if one type of evidence fails to convince the court, another type might succeed.

§6.2.2. Types of Evidence.

What type of evidence should the advocate offer to support the factual assertions in a minor premise? It depends. In an appeal, for example, the universe of available evidence is generally limited to the factual findings of the trial court contained in the record.

In a trial court, the nature of acceptable evidence varies greatly with the context. For purposes of a motion to dismiss, for instance, the allegations of the complaint must be taken as true and constitute the only source of evidence. After the pleadings have closed, in contrast, only those allegations in the complaint admitted by the defendant are considered to be true.

In a summary judgment motion, the advocate may rely on any evidence that would be admissible at trial. Such evidence might include affidavits, authenticated or uncontested exhibits, discovery responses, and stipulated facts. In a post-trial brief, the available evidence consists of any evidence admitted at trial, including testimony. Where questions of collateral estoppel or res judicata arise, the factual findings of other courts may sometimes constitute conclusive evidence.

Some factual assertions may require no additional grounding in evidence because they are so obviously true that any attempt to support them would seem ludicrous ("The sky is blue," "Adults are older than children," "People need money to live," etc.). Technically, such facts are established by judicial notice. In practice, however, nobody wastes the court's time asking it to take judicial notice of such banalities. Instead, lawyers simply assert such facts without evidentiary support and courts accept them, provided of course that opposing counsel never openly disputes them.

§ 6.2.3. Appeals to Common Sense.

In our legal system, factual disputes are supposed to be settled by a fact finder after consideration of the evidence. In practice, however, many factual issues are resolved by appeals to common sense unsupported by evidence. Lawyers appeal to common sense primarily in two instances.

First, an appeal to common sense may represent a simple inference from facts that are unstated because they are obviously true or are otherwise undisputed. If it rains today, common sense will tell you that the picnic should be canceled. You need no further explanation of the relationship between rain, picnicking and recreational enjoyment in order to accept the logical link between the two events.

The second kind of appeal to common sense occurs in an ill-defined class of cases in which the court interprets the law or deliberates on legal policy in a way that requires it to make factual assumptions about the world. For example, the fourth amendment requires a police officer to obtain a warrant before searching any place in which a person has a sufficiently strong "expectation of privacy." The Supreme Court has held, by and large, that people in automobiles have a diminished expectation of privacy. But the Court has not decided these questions on the basis of testimony by people who drive cars, or on the basis of studies of public attitudes by social scientists. Rather, the Court has ruled on the basis of its "common sense" view of how people use cars and behave in them.

Many other issues are decided in the same way. Does a law allowing public officials to bring libel suits against newspapers "chill" free speech? Will an erosion of the spousal privilege against giving testimony lead to the dissolution of marriages? Will a state law requiring trucks to have certain kinds of mud flaps impose a burden on interstate commerce? In all of these cases, courts have relied on common sense rather than provable facts.

From the advocate's point of view, these kinds of appeals to common sense are nothing more than factual assertions that either are not or cannot be grounded in evidence. Thus, in the appropriate kind of case, the advocate may choose to leave a factual assertion ungrounded by anything other than its own intrinsic plausibility. However, that does not mean that the advocate should not *try* to ground the assertion in evidence if good evidence is available. Even factual assertions that seem plausible on their face can be made more persuasive if supported by evidence.

§ 6.3. Establish Certainty of Content By Using Brute Facts.

§ 6.3.1. Brute Facts and Compound Facts.

Not all factual assertions are equally persuasive, even when they are supported by evidence of equivalent weight and reliability. Suppose the same person told you the following two things:

A. I have a headache.
B. I just saw Stella cheating on her husband.

Most people would be inclined to accept statement A as true automatically, but would be reluctant to accept statement B as true without further explanation. They might want to know more about the circumstances of the observation, such as the time and place, as well as information about who Stella was with, and what Stella did to make the speaker think she was cheating.

These two statements illustrate the difference between *brute facts* and *compound facts*. Brute facts are facts about the physical world – what someone did or said or perceived, or the physical location or condition of an object. They are first-order reports concerning physical reality. Compound facts, in contrast, combine reports concerning the physical world with inferences based on those facts. It may be a "fact" that Stella was cheating on her husband, but that fact can only be known through a process of inference based on other facts concerning marriage, social conventions, and the specifics of Stella's behavior.

Assertions of brute fact are intrinsically more persuasive than assertions of compound fact. Just about the only reason why a listener would reject an assertion of brute fact is the listener's mistrust of the speaker – that is, the listener thinks the speaker is either a liar or an unreliable reporter. Because people who report having headaches rarely have a reason to lie, and can hardly be mistaken about whether they have a headache, we ordinarily accept complaints about headaches as true.

In contrast, a listener might reject an assertion of compound fact for reasons having nothing to do with the speaker's trustworthiness. The listener might, for example, feel that the speaker has drawn a faulty inference from otherwise reliable data. Thus, we might reject a friend's assertion that Stella was cheating on her husband not because we doubt the friend's report that Stella was in the company of another man, but because we doubt the validity of the friend's inference that Stella's behavior amounted to cheating.

For these reasons, the advocate should fashion minor premises out of brute facts whenever possible.

§6.3.2. Break Down Compound Facts Into Brute Facts.

Sometimes it is impossible to construct a minor premise out of brute facts. Either the conclusion to which the advocate is committed or the language of the controlling legal rule (or both) can make the use of compound factual assertions unavoidable. Even in these circumstances, however, the advocate can still reap the advantages offered by brute facts by *breaking down* any compound facts and grounding them indirectly in their constituent brute facts.

For example, the compound assertion "I saw Stella cheating on her husband" might be made far more persuasive by breaking it down into some of the following brute facts:

1. Stella's husband is Ted.
2. I saw Stella with John.
3. They were in a restaurant having dinner.
4. They were holding hands.
5. When I walked by, Stella blushed and pretended not to see me.

Following is a more complicated, legal example. Suppose we represent the plaintiff in a workplace health and safety lawsuit in which the plaintiff claims that she was injured by exposure in her employer's factory to dangerous levels of benzene. We have retained an expert to testify on the plaintiff's behalf.

Suppose further that, in light of the law and our position in the case, we have no choice but to advance as a minor premise of our argument the following proposition:

2. The plaintiff was exposed to dangerous levels of benzene in the factory.

We could directly ground this assertion simply by citing to the equivalent language in our expert's affidavit, and, indeed, we should do so:

2. The plaintiff was exposed to dangerous levels of benzene in the factory. Affidavit of Dr. Barbara Post, ¶ 6.

This premise is now directly grounded, and a factual assertion of any kind always has a certain persuasiveness when it is directly grounded in evidence. Nevertheless, the premise is not as persuasive as it could be because it contains an assertion of compound fact. To say that the benzene levels at issue were "dangerous" is to draw an inference from other facts concerning acceptable levels of benzene exposure and the amount of benzene to which the plaintiff was exposed.

We can make this premise more persuasive by breaking it down and grounding it in its constituent brute facts. Here is one possibility:

1. Ambient benzene levels exceeding 1.5 parts per million are dangerous. United States Occupational Health and Safety Administration, Official Workplace Guidelines (Exhibit 1), p. 248.
2. Ambient benzene levels in the plaintiff's factory average 3 parts per million. Report of Chemical Technician Russell Brand (Exhibit 2), p. 4.
3. Therefore, the plaintiff was exposed to dangerous levels of benzene in the factory.

The minor premise of this syllogism is an assertion of brute fact – it makes a claim about the physical world. The overall persuasiveness of the original factual premise has thus been slightly increased because the minor premise of the new syllogism can be rejected only if the court is given some reason to doubt the physical observations of Chemical Technician Russell Brand.

The major premise still seems to contain an assertion of compound fact, and we now face a decision: should we leave the premise grounded in evidence of official federal guidelines, or should we break it down further? As always, the degree to which a premise should be considered grounded depends upon the context. If in the circumstances of the case the court is likely to accept the federal guidelines as authoritative then there is little reason to go on. If, on the other hand, the conclusions contained in the guidelines themselves require justification, we must continue the process of breaking down the compound facts into their brute constituents.

As a general rule, however, when you are unsure about whether a particular compound factual statement is fully grounded, the best practice is to err on the side of caution and break it down more completely into brute facts.

§ 6.4. Elaborate Key Legal Terms.

§ 6.4.1. Legal Aspects of the Minor Premise.

The minor premise of a legal syllogism is rarely a pure statement of fact. Because the minor premise applies law to fact, it usually contains elements of both. We have now seen how to ground the factual aspects of a minor premise. What do we do with the legal aspects?

Because syllogisms are based on the transitivity principle (§ 1.3), every premise of every syllogism declares two things to be equivalent. In a legal syllogism, the minor premise always declares a particular kind of equivalence: it asserts the equivalence of a legal concept and a set of facts. Law and fact, however, seem like very different things. Legal rules and concepts are often vague and abstract, whereas facts are necessarily concrete. How can two such different things be shown to be equivalent? More specifically, how is it possible to show the equivalence of something vague and something concrete?

There are only two ways to accomplish this task. Either we must bring the facts up to the level of abstraction and vagueness of the law, or we must bring the law down to the level of concreteness of the facts. The first possibility is unacceptable because, as we have seen, facts are more persuasive when they are concrete, and the advocate's job is, after all, to persuade. It follows that we must somehow present the pertinent legal concepts contained in the minor premise so as to make them seem every bit as concrete as the facts themselves. The advocate can do this by *elaborating the key legal terms* of the minor premise.

The elaboration of key legal terms is a two-step process. First, the advocate must identify the critical terms. Second, the advocate must ground these legal terms in concrete legal explanations of their meaning.

§ 6.4.2. Identify the Key Terms.

Which legal terms in a minor premise must be elaborated? Generally, any legal term that is not self-explanatory ought to be elaborated. However, at a minimum, the advocate must almost always elaborate the *common term* – the legal term appearing in the minor premise that also appears in the major premise.

Here are some examples of legal syllogisms with the common term indicated:

1. In order to be enforceable, a contract must be supported by consideration.
2. The contract between Tim and Mary is supported by *consideration*.

3. Therefore, the contract between Tim and Mary is enforceable.

1. A defendant is not liable for a plaintiff's injuries if the plaintiff assumed the risk of injury.
2. The plaintiff in this case *assumed the risk* of injury.
3. Therefore, the defendant is not liable in this case.

1. Fighting words are not protected by the first amendment.
2. John's words were *fighting words*.
3. Therefore, John's words were not protected by the first amendment.

Each of the terms indicated above must be elaborated to assure the persuasiveness of the minor premise in which it appears. That these terms require elaboration should come as no surprise. "Consideration," "assumption of risk" and "fighting words" are all legal terms of art. If the advocate is to demonstrate persuasively that these terms have been correctly applied to the facts of the case, the advocate must clarify their meaning.

§ 6.4.3. Tell the Judge: "Here's How You Know It When You See It."

After identifying the legal terms in need of elaboration, the advocate must perform the elaboration. The precise nature and content of the required elaboration may vary from one context to another, but the advocate can never go wrong if he or she follows this rule. For any legal term to be elaborated, explain to the judge: *"Here's how you know it when you see it."*

Let's take an example. Suppose you represent Frank in a contract dispute with Judy. Frank mentioned to Judy one day that he didn't use his beach house very much, and would consider selling it if he could get $50,000. The next day, Judy presented Frank with a check for $50,000, which he refused. Judy now claims that Frank breached a contract to sell her the house.

Suppose you wish to argue to the court that there was never any contract between Frank and Judy because Frank never made a valid offer to sell. You need to persuade the court to accept the following minor premise:

2. Frank did not make an offer.

Imagine the following dialogue between you and the judge:

YOU: Your Honor, Frank did not make an offer to sell his house to Judy.

JUDGE: So you say, counsel, but I'll make up my own mind on that issue, thank you very much. How do I know that your client didn't make an offer? How do I know an "offer" when I see one?

What can you tell the judge to answer this question? Clearly, you must explain to the court just what an "offer" is. You must define or elaborate the term in a way that permits the judge to see exactly why no offer is present in this case.

To do this, you must clarify in your own mind precisely why you think there was no offer. Suppose you think your premise is true because you have found a case in which the highest court in the jurisdiction ruled that the term "offer" means "the manifestation of willingness to enter into a bargain." Since Frank said only that he would be willing to *consider* selling his house for $50,000, and not that he would definitely do so, his statement to Judy did not show the necessary willingness to enter into a contract to sell his house and thus could not have been an offer.

You can now answer the judge's challenge:

YOU: How do you know an "offer" when you see one? Well, an "offer" means "the manifestation of willingness to enter into a bargain." If you are looking at a manifestation of willingness to enter into a bargain, Your Honor, then you are looking at an offer.

Let's put this information into the form of a syllogistic argument. Here is the original syllogism that contains the minor premise in need of legal elaboration:

1. The alleged contract between Frank and Judy could not have been formed unless Frank made an offer. *Gaines v. Humboldt.*
2. Frank did not make an offer.
3. Therefore, no contract was formed between Frank and Judy.

Now convert the minor premise to the conclusion of a new syllogism:

1.
2.
3. Therefore, Frank did not make an offer.

Fill in the premises of this new syllogism, elaborating the meaning of the legal term "offer":

1. An offer is the manifestation of willingness to enter into a bargain.
2. Frank did not manifest willingness to enter into a bargain.
3. Therefore, Frank did not make an offer.

Finally, ground the premises in law or fact, as appropriate. The major premise can be grounded in case authority; the minor premise can perhaps be grounded in an affidavit by Frank in which he relates his exact words and intentions during his conversation with Judy:

1. An offer is the manifestation of willingness to enter into a bargain. *James v. Kenney*.
2. Frank did not manifest willingness to enter into a bargain. Affidavit of Frank, ¶ 5.
3. Therefore, Frank did not make an offer.

The original minor premise is now fully grounded in both its legal and factual aspects. The complete chain of grounding is shown in the following diagram.

1. The alleged contract between Frank and Judy could not have been formed unless Frank made an offer. *Gaines v. Humboldt*.
2. Frank did not make an offer. →
3. Therefore, no contract was formed between Frank and Judy.

1. An offer is the manifestation of willingness to enter into a bargain. *James v. Kenney*.
2. Frank did not manifest willingness to enter into a bargain. Affidavit of Frank, ¶ 5.
3. Therefore, Frank did not make an offer.

We can perform the same type of elaboration for other legal terms. Suppose we represent the defendant in a tort suit and we wish to argue that our client is not liable for the plaintiff's injury because the plaintiff assumed the risk:

1. A defendant is not liable for a plaintiff's injuries if the plaintiff assumed the risk of injury. *Lawson v. Moore.*
2. The plaintiff assumed the risk of injury.
3. Therefore, the defendant is not liable.

Here, the common term in need of elaboration is "assumption of risk," another legal term of art. How do we know assumption of risk when we see it? Suppose legal research tells us that a person assumes the risk of injury by expressly agreeing to do so. We could thus ground the minor premise by elaborating the key term as follows:

1. A person assumes the risk of injury by expressly agreeing to do so. *Nelson v. Otto.*
2. The plaintiff expressly agreed to assume the risk of injury.
3. Therefore, the plaintiff assumed the risk of injury.

Note that our elaboration of the legal term has left us with a syllogism that can be fully grounded simply by grounding the minor premise in evidence. We have told the judge what to look for – an express agreement – and we need only supply evidence of such an express agreement in order to win the case.

§ 6.5. Conclusory Argument.

By far the most common error in legal advocacy is *conclusory* argument. An advocate's argument is conclusory when the advocate fails to spell out each step in his or her reasoning, or makes assertions about the law or the facts without backing them up – in other words, a conclusory argument is one that is inadequately grounded. No matter how internally logical and externally truthful it may be, a conclusory argument will never be persuasive because it fails to demonstrate why the court should accept its premises as true.

A typical conclusory argument might go something like this:

> Under the equal protection clause, legislative classifications that treat members of a "suspect class" worse than members of other groups must survive "strict scrutiny." *Sugarman v. Dougall.* A class of individuals constitutes a suspect class within the meaning of the equal protection clause if it is the subject of stereotypes, if it faces discrimination in society, and if its members are lumped together on the basis of immutable characteristics that bear no relation to the members' ability to perform or contribute to society. *Frontiero v. Richardson.* The elderly are such a group. They are subject to many stereotypes, they are victims of persistent discrimination, and they are grouped according to an immutable characteristic unrelated to their contribution to society. Consequently, the elderly are a suspect class.

What makes this passage conclusory is its failure to back up its assertions about the elderly, assertions which, if true, have significant legal consequences. For example, the passage claims that the elderly are subject to stereotypes. This may be true, but just what are the stereotypes? A reader who does not already think that there are such stereotypes can hardly be persuaded of their existence because not a single stereotype is identified. Similarly, the assertion about discrimination against the elderly is completely unsupported by *any* facts, evidence or examples, and is thus entirely unpersuasive.

Nine times out of ten, conclusory argument results from inadequate grounding of the minor premise. And in most of these cases, advocates fail to ground the premise adequately because they incorrectly believe that their reasoning will be so obvious to the court that no further explanation is required.

Advocates generally believe that their reasoning will be obvious to the court even without adequate grounding for one of two reasons. The first reason is that the advocate erroneously assumes that the court is so knowledgeable and so intelligent that thorough grounding of the minor premise is superfluous. This error shows up most commonly in a failure to elaborate key legal terms. Many beginning law students (and, sadly, many lawyers) assume that the court knows the law inside and out, and that elaboration of key legal concepts is unnecessary. Some may even think that an advocate's detailed elaboration of the law is somehow insulting to the court.

Nothing could be further from the truth. First, judges often do not know the relevant law, or know it only vaguely, or cannot recall the details instantaneously. These judges are grateful to the advocate for any and all exposition of the law. Second, even judges who know the law thoroughly will not be fully persuaded unless they understand each step in the advocate's legal reasoning. Good judges are skeptics, and skeptics are unlikely to accept even the most attractive premises as true unless they are convinced that the premises rest on sound foundations.

The same type of reasoning may also lead advocates to fail to ground the factual assertions contained in their minor premises. Surely, they may think, a learned judge can grasp the facts of the case after a cursory description, kept conveniently short by using as many compound facts as possible. Not so. Judges are often intelligent, but not always, and even intelligent judges are human; one persuades them as one would persuade anybody else. If brute facts are more persuasive than compound facts, then the advocate should present brute facts to the court, and the more the better. Legal advocacy is not a game of "chicken"; the advocate should not strive to win by coming as close as possible to the precipice of failure.

The second common reason why advocates fail to ground their minor premises adequately is their erroneous assumption that the truth of a premise is self-evident. Merely to understand the proposition, they erroneously assume, is to accept it.

Many legal and factual propositions are self-evidently true, to be sure – but not nearly so many as their proponents believe. One of the occupational hazards of professional advocacy is a certain kind of blindness. One who lives with an argument day after day, honing and refining it and defending it against all attacks, can easily lose the ability to evaluate objectively the strength of contrary or alternative arguments.

Advocates should always be aware of this danger and should accordingly try to maintain a healthy skepticism toward the persuasive power of their arguments. If a premise seems self-evident to you, doubt yourself. You can never harm your chances of success by thorough grounding. If the premise really *is* self-evidently true, then no amount of grounding can make it any the less so. If the premise is *not* self-evidently true, then it must be grounded if the court is to accept it, so any effort spent grounding the premise is well worthwhile.

§ 6.6. A Grounded Minor Premise Guides Factual Development.

A fully grounded minor premise is not only essential to a persuasive argument in the advanced stages of a case, but can also help the advocate in the earliest stages of case preparation. Because a minor premise must be grounded in facts, a grounded minor premise provides a blueprint for the advocate's investigation and collection of the evidence.

To take advantage of this benefit, the advocate must speculate a bit. After performing the necessary legal research and elaborating key legal terms, the advocate must ask: what evidence could possibly enable me to ground this syllogism? The advocate should attempt to answer this question thoroughly and creatively, hypothesizing multiple groundings whenever possible. Only then should the advocate take whatever steps are necessary, including conducting investigations and taking discovery, to see if the desired evidence really exists. Such preparation sharpens discovery and makes blind "fishing expeditions" largely unnecessary. And sharper discovery, of course, reduces litigation costs.

Chapter 7

SUMMARY OF THE METHOD (A STEP-BY-STEP ANALYSIS)

Below is a summary in step-by-step format of the method set out in the preceding chapters for constructing a persuasive legal argument in syllogistic form.

STEP 1:

Determine your client's alignment in the case (generally plaintiff or defendant).

STEP 2:

Identify the legal principles relevant to the case (e.g., contract law, tort law, equal protection).

STEP 3:

Generate a set of presumptive positions by taking the side favorable to your client or unfavorable to your opponent on every potentially relevant legal principle.

STEP 4:

From the set of presumptive positions select your actual positions by eliminating any presumptive positions that are false, unpersuasive, excessively complex, unsupported by the facts, or unsuitable for any other reason.

STEP 5:

Formulate your position on the relief sought in the case. Make this position the centerpiece of your argument. Where the relief in issue is not the relief ultimately sought in the case, but the relief sought in a particular motion, formulate your position on the relief sought in the motion.

STEP 6:

Convert each position into the conclusion of a syllogism.

STEP 7:

Construct the premises of each syllogism using a recursive process of trial and error. This process should be guided by the following considerations:

1. The premises must yield the desired conclusion;
2. All terms of the syllogism must match;
3. The specification of any two terms specifies the third;
4. The premises must be true;
5. Major premises should use the language of tests, steps or factors; and
6. Minor premises should assert brute facts.

STEP 8:

Ground the major premise directly in controlling authority (case law, statutes, constitutions, etc.). If the major premise cannot be directly grounded, ground it indirectly by converting the premise to the conclusion of a new syllogism and constructing a new set of premises that can be directly grounded. Continue this process until all legal premises are directly grounded in controlling authority.

STEP 9:

Ground factual aspects of the minor premise directly in evidence. If the premise cannot be so grounded, ground it indirectly by converting the premise to the conclusion of a new syllogism and constructing a new set of premises that can be directly grounded. Continue this process until all factual assertions are directly grounded in evidence.

STEP 10:

Break down assertions of compound fact in the minor premise into their constituent brute facts by grounding them indirectly in evidence of the underlying brute facts.

STEP 11:

Elaborate key legal terms in the minor premise by grounding them indirectly in explanations of their legal meaning.

STEP 12:

Continue in the same manner until all premises are fully grounded.

Chapter 8

PUTTING TOGETHER A COMPLETE ARGUMENT

§ 8.1. Introduction.
§ 8.2. The Facts.
§ 8.3. The Law.
§ 8.4. The Argument.

§ 8.1. Introduction.

This chapter illustrates the method set out in the preceding pages by constructing a complete set of interlocking, grounded syllogistic arguments based on the law and facts of a hypothetical case. The case at issue is an employment case in which the plaintiff, a female who has been fired by a small company, alleges that she was fired because of her gender. We shall focus on a question of civil procedure. The plaintiff, who has maintained the suit for over three years solely as an employment discrimination case, now seeks to amend her complaint to add new causes of action based on fraud and breach of contract. We represent the defendant company. Our objective is to persuade the court to deny the plaintiff's motion to amend her complaint.

§ 8.2. The Facts.

Alice King was employed as an assembly line worker by the Eastern Tool Company (ETC), of Concord, Massachusetts. After about eighteen months, ETC fired King. ETC claimed that King was fired because she was incompetent; King claimed that she was fired because of gender discrimination. Three years ago, she filed suit against ETC in the United States District Court for the District of Massachusetts. Her complaint alleged a single count of gender discrimination under Title VII, a federal anti-discrimination law.

In response to the complaint, ETC took extensive discovery, including two sets of interrogatories, two sets of requests for production of documents, six depositions, and a set of requests for admission. ETC completed its discovery some twenty months ago. King also appears to have completed her discovery; in any event, she has not sought any additional discovery in nearly two years. The court has not yet scheduled the case for trial, and King has not moved the court to set a trial date.

King has now filed a motion to amend her complaint. According to her motion, she wishes to add new state law claims based on fraud and breach of contract. The only explanation that King offers in support of her motion to amend is the following: "Further review of the law and facts shows that plaintiff has additional state law claims in fraud and breach of contract."

§ 8.3. The Law.

We need to do two kinds of research. First, we need to find out generally about the conditions under which plaintiffs may amend their complaints. Second, we need to find cases like this one, in which the motion to amend is made very late in the game, preferably after the close of discovery. The most useful cases would come from the First Circuit. Suppose we perform the research and find, in brief, the following.

Motions to amend pleadings in federal court are governed by Rule 15(a) of the Federal Rules of Civil Procedure, which provides:

> A party may amend the party's pleading once as a matter of course at any time before a responsive

> pleading is served . . . . Otherwise a party may amend the party's pleading only by leave of court . . . ; and leave shall be freely given when justice so requires.

Since an answer has already been filed and we do not consent to the amendment, the plaintiff can amend her complaint only with leave of court. Unfortunately, the rule suggests that leave should be freely granted. Assuming that even this broad language does not mean that every motion to amend should be granted, we need to find out when a court can properly deny leave to amend.

The leading Supreme Court case interpreting Rule 15(a) is *Foman v. Davis*. In *Foman,* the Court said that leave to amend may be denied in four situations: "undue delay, bad faith or dilatory motive on the part of the movant, repeated failure to cure deficiencies by amendments previously allowed, [and] undue prejudice to the opposing party by virtue of allowance of the amendment." We can eliminate two of these at once: we have no reason to suspect bad faith, and this is the first attempt to amend. That leaves "undue delay" and "prejudice." But this is all still very vague. What we need is authority refining the Court's *Foman* formulation into some kind of concrete test.

Further research shows that the Supreme Court has said almost nothing about Rule 15(a) since *Foman,* so we need to consult the lower courts. Here, we're in luck. In *Manzoli v. Commissioner of Internal Revenue,* the First Circuit said: "an untimely amendment request should be denied where . . . no excuse for delay existed and . . . the adverse party would suffer prejudice or substantial inconvenience." We can argue that this language states a two-part test, which we can satisfy: plaintiff has no excuse, and ETC would suffer prejudice.

Our next task is to elaborate the key terms of each prong of the test: we need to clarify what constitutes an "excuse" for delay in this Circuit, and what constitutes "prejudice" within the meaning of *Manzoli* or *Foman*. Further research shows that the First Circuit has never clearly defined the concept of excusable delay for untimely amendments. However, the court has said something almost as good. According to the court in *Hayes v. New England Millwork,* where "a considerable period of time has passed between the filing of the complaint and the motion to amend," the courts place the burden on the plaintiff to show a "valid reason for his neglect and delay." We can take advantage of this shift in burden because the plaintiff's motion basically gives no reason for the delay. Furthermore, *Hayes* makes clear that simple neglect is not a valid excuse. Perhaps we can suggest that neglect is what's really going on here.

That brings us to the second prong of the *Manzoli* test: the meaning of "prejudice." Again, the court has not set out a neat test for prejudice. But let's try a different approach – let's work backwards from the facts. Why do we feel like our client will be "prejudiced" if the plaintiff's motion is granted? The reason is easy to pin down: if the plaintiff amends her complaint, ETC will have had no opportunity to develop a defense to her new claims. That means we need to take new discovery, which means additional time and expense. Those are the facts we have to work with. If we are going to be able to show prejudice at all, then being forced to delay the case by reopening discovery must fall within the legal definition of prejudice.

Is there First Circuit authority that could support such an argument? Fortunately, there is. In *Manzoli,* the court found prejudice where the parties would have had to create a "new record," and in *Hayes,* the court found prejudice where the defendant would have been forced to defend new claims after the close of discovery. Let's argue that these cases state a rule of law – a defendant would suffer prejudice by being forced to defend new claims after the close of discovery – and that ETC falls within the rule.

There is one more thing we ought to do: if possible, we should try to find a case that is as factually similar to our case as possible, *and* in which the court denied leave to amend.[6] Some First Circuit cases are close, but not identical. There is, however, a nearly identical case from the Seventh Circuit, *Amendola v. Bayer,* with the proper result. Authority from another circuit is good enough in a pinch, so we can keep *Amendola* in reserve as a bolstering analogy (see §9.2.4).

§8.4. The Argument.

Now let's construct the syllogistic argument. First we note our client's alignment. Although ETC is the defendant in the case, we are concerned at the moment with a motion rather than the ultimate merits of the case. As a result, the alignment relevant here is that we oppose the motion (§2.6.2). Next we determine what legal principles might apply. As we already know, Rule 15(a) of the Federal Rules of Civil Procedure applies, along with its judicial interpretations by the Supreme Court and First Circuit. From here we can generate a set of presumptive positions. In light of the applicable law, our presumptive positions might include the following:

1. Plaintiff's motion must be denied;
2. Rule 15(a) requires denial of plaintiff's motion;
3. Granting plaintiff's motion would unduly prejudice defendant;

---

[6] Notice how much research is required to do a thorough and persuasive job of arguing even the simplest question of civil procedure.

4. Plaintiff has offered no excuse for her delay in moving to amend;
5. If plaintiff's motion were granted, defendant would have to conduct new discovery.

Obviously, we could generate more presumptive positions, but perhaps we can stop here given that we are dealing, for the moment at least, with some relatively specific issues to be raised in our opposition to a motion for specific relief.

From this set of presumptive positions we must now discard any that might be unsuitable for actual use. At this point, none of the positions seems particularly weak, so let's provisionally keep them all.

The next step is to begin converting our positions to the conclusions of syllogisms. Here are some of the conclusions we might generate:

1.
2.
3. Therefore, plaintiff's motion must be denied.

1.
2.
3. Therefore, granting plaintiff's motion would unduly prejudice defendant.

1.
2.
3. Therefore, plaintiff has offered no valid excuse for her delay in moving to amend.

Now we must fill in these syllogisms by constructing the premises. Because this is an argument opposing a motion, let's begin with the first of these three syllogisms because it deals with the outcome to the motion that we seek. How can we fill in the premises? We must ask ourselves: why do we think that this motion should be denied? Based on our evaluation of the law and facts, we believe the motion must be denied because the plaintiff has offered no excuse for her delay, and because granting the motion would cause defendant undue prejudice:

1. A Rule 15(a) motion to amend a complaint must be denied if (1) the plaintiff has offered no excuse for delay, and (2) the adverse party would suffer prejudice.
2. The plaintiff has offered no excuse for delay, and the adverse party would suffer prejudice.
3. Therefore, this motion must be denied.

This is a winning syllogism. If the court accepts the premises as true, then it will have no choice but to deny the motion, as we wish. However, the syllogism is far from persuasive because it is totally ungrounded. How can we ground it?

The major premise can be directly grounded by citations to Rule 15(a), *Foman* and *Manzoli*. The minor premise presents greater difficulty. The main problem is that it contains two key legal terms – "excuse" and "prejudice" – that must be elaborated. Let's do so by indirectly grounding the premise in an elaboration of each critical term. Because each term must be separately elaborated, our syllogistic structure must bifurcate at this point. Let's start with the excuse prong. We begin the process of indirectly grounding the premise by converting the relevant portion of the minor premise to the conclusion of a new syllogism:

1.
2.
3. Therefore, plaintiff has offered no excuse for delay.

Now let's elaborate the meaning of "excuse." Remember, we did not discover a comprehensive legal definition of valid excuses; rather, the courts shift the burden onto the plaintiff to offer such an excuse:

1. To assert an excuse for delay in filing an untimely motion to amend, the plaintiff must show a "valid reason for his neglect and delay." *Hayes*
2. Plaintiff has not shown any valid reason for her neglect and delay.
3. Therefore, plaintiff has offered no excuse for delay.

The major premise can be grounded with a citation to *Hayes,* which leaves us with a minor premise in need of grounding. Ordinarily, we might want to ground such a minor premise further by elaborating the key legal term "valid reason." Here, however, the plaintiff has offered essentially no reason at all, so it really doesn't matter what constitutes a valid reason: one who offers no reason certainly cannot have offered a valid reason. Thus, we can treat this premise as requiring only factual grounding in evidence – here, the evidence would come from Plaintiff's Motion to Amend itself:

2. Plaintiff has not shown any valid reason for her neglect and delay. Plaintiff's Motion to Amend Complaint at 1.

If we are still uncomfortable about not providing a legal definition of "valid reason" there is one additional thing we can do. Although the cases do not give us a test for distinguishing valid reasons from invalid ones, they do provide some specific examples of valid and invalid reasons.

For example, the Fourth Circuit has held that a valid reason for delaying a motion to amend is the discovery of new evidence. *Island Creek Coal Co. v. Lake Shore, Inc.* We can point out that the plaintiff has not claimed that she discovered new evidence, so she has not offered at least one possible valid reason for her untimely motion. Similarly, the First Circuit in *Hayes* said that allowing one's case to "lie fallow" is not a valid reason for an untimely motion to amend. We may be able to suggest to the court that the plaintiff's real reason for the delay is this kind of neglect, and plaintiff's reason is therefore not a valid one.

The following syllogism might do the trick:

1. Allowing one's case to "lie fallow" for a lengthy period is not a valid reason for filing an untimely motion to amend. *Hayes*.
2. Plaintiff has allowed her case to lie fallow.
3. Therefore, plaintiff has not offered a valid reason for her neglect and delay.

This leaves us with the problem of how to ground the minor premise. We obviously have no direct evidence of what the plaintiff has been doing for the last two years. However, we have circumstantial evidence to support our speculation that she has done nothing. First, she has neither taken discovery nor moved for a trial date. Those are just about the only things that an active litigant would be doing during the late stages of a case like this. Second, we can draw a negative inference from the fact that the plaintiff has not claimed, for example, to have discovered new evidence, something that would constitute a valid excuse. That is, we can ask the court to infer that because the plaintiff has not claimed to have discovered new evidence, she must not have done so;

had she found something new, she would have said so. Of course, the plaintiff may be able to rebut this inference by showing that she has in fact discovered new evidence – but that's her problem, not ours. Thus, we may ground the minor premise of the preceding syllogism in evidence of what the plaintiff has done, and also what she hasn't done:

2. Plaintiff has allowed her case to lie fallow. *See* Motion to Amend Complaint, *Hayes*; *compare Island Creek Coal.*

Now let's return to the "prejudice" prong. Again, we begin the process of indirect grounding by converting the relevant portion of the original minor premise to the conclusion of a new syllogism:

1.
2.
3. Therefore, defendant would suffer prejudice.

Now let's elaborate the meaning of "prejudice":

1. A defendant would suffer prejudice by being forced to defend new claims after the close of discovery. *Hayes.*
2. Defendant would have to defend new claims after the close of discovery.
3. Therefore, defendant would suffer prejudice.

It is now a simple matter to ground the minor premise. Nobody seems to dispute that discovery on the original Title VII claim has closed. We thus need to show only that we would have to defend "new claims" if the motion to amend is granted. Again, we could perform further legal grounding of the syllogism by offering a legal definition of the term "new claims," but it will probably be self-evident to most judges that gender discrimination claims are quite different from fraud and breach of contract claims. It follows that we may consider the minor premise of this syllogism fully grounded merely by citing to the plaintiff's motion to amend.

The following diagram shows the entire argument developed above. The syllogisms are numbered for reference. We shall return to these syllogisms in §9.4, where they will be converted into a complete brief.

1

1. A Rule 15(a) motion to amend a complaint must be denied if (1) the plaintiff has offered no excuse for delay, and (2) the adverse party would suffer prejudice. FED. R. CIV. P. 15(a); *Foman; Manzoli*.
2. The plaintiff has offered no excuse for delay, and the adverse party would suffer prejudice.
3. Therefore, this motion must be denied.

2

1. To assert an excuse for delay in filing an untimely motion to amend, the plaintiff must show a "valid reason for his neglect and delay." *Hayes*.
2. Plaintiff has not shown any valid reason for her neglect and delay. Plaintiff's Motion to Amend Complaint at 1.
3. Therefore, plaintiff has offered no excuse for delay.

3

1. Allowing one's case to "lie fallow" for a lengthy period is not a valid reason for filing an untimely motion to amend. *Hayes*.
2. Plaintiff has allowed her case to lie fallow. *See* Motion to Amend Complaint, *Hayes*; *compare Island Creek Coal*.
3. Therefore, plaintiff has not shown any valid reason for her neglect and delay.

4

1. A defendant would suffer prejudice by being forced to defend new claims after the close of discovery. *Haynes*.
2. Defendant would have to defend new claims after the close of discovery. Plaintiff's Motion to Amend Complaint.
3. Therefore, defendant would suffer prejudice.

Chapter 9

WRITING A LEGAL ARGUMENT

§ 9.1. A Formula For Writing Arguments.
§ 9.2. Elements of the Formula.
  § 9.2.1. The Set-Up.
  § 9.2.2. Setting Out the Law.
  § 9.2.3. Apply the Law to the Facts.
  § 9.2.4. Bolster With Analogous Precedent.
§ 9.3. Clarity Always Takes Precedence.
§ 9.4. An Example of Reducing an Argument to Writing.
  § 9.4.1. The Outline.
  § 9.4.2. The Brief.

§ 9.1. A Formula for Writing Arguments.

An advocate obviously cannot file with the court a diagram of nested syllogisms; the advocate must convert the argument from a set of interlocking concepts into a smoothly written legal brief. Because the primary goal of briefwriting is clarity, the organization of the brief is dictated less by the conceptual structure of the particular arguments advanced than by the requirements of good writing. Our inquiry, then, must focus on the best and clearest way to write a legal argument.

Many lawyers and teachers of legal writing maintain that every argument is unique and every brief is different; it is therefore impossible, they claim, to reduce the art of briefwriting to a formula. This is nonsense. Any experienced litigator must admit that few things in the practice of law are quite so formulaic as the writing of briefs. Every now and then, of course, a brief will come along that presents some unique difficulty requiring a novel approach, but the vast majority of legal arguments can be and are written in a predictable way.

Below is an outline for the written presentation of a legal argument. Each element of the outline is explained further in the next section.

1. Set-up
   a. Identify your target
   b. State your conclusion
2. Set out the law
   a. Identify and introduce relevant doctrines or provisions
   b. Explicate the law
      i. Provide context
      ii. Explain purpose
   c. Set out the controlling test, step analysis, or factor analysis
3. Apply the law to the facts
4. Bolster with analogous precedent.

Two points must be borne in mind when using this formula. First, the formula covers only legal arguments presented in the argument section of a brief; it does not cover other parts of briefs, such as the introduction or statement of facts. Second, the formula applies to the presentation of a single, distinct argument or sub-argument. The formula does not address the integration of multiple arguments into a coherent whole.

§ 9.2. Elements of the Formula.

§ 9.2.1. The Set-Up.

The set-up serves as an introduction to the argument. It focuses the court's attention on the nature of the argument and reveals in advance the conclusion the advocate intends to support. Providing this information at the immediate outset of the argument allows the court to follow the argument more easily because the court knows in advance where the advocate is headed.

A. *Identification of the Target*

The first element of the set-up is the identification of your target. Every legal argument is an attack. The plaintiff always attacks either the defendant's actions, contending they were illegal, or the defendant's arguments in defense of those actions, contending they are wrong. Similarly, the defendant always attacks the plaintiff's theories of liability and supporting arguments as legally or factually incorrect.

Because an argument is an attack, you must make clear to the court precisely what is being attacked. The most skillful dismantling of an opponent's position will be lost on a court that misses the action because its attention is focused elsewhere. The advocate should say to the court, in essence: "Your Honor – see that argument over there? Well, watch closely, because I am about to demolish it."

This portion of the set-up can usually be accomplished in a single sentence. Here are some examples of opening a legal argument by identifying the target to be attacked:

> On October 10, 1991, defendant informed plaintiff that it would not make payment under the terms of the June 15, 1991 contract.

> Plaintiff alleges in Count One of the complaint that the city's failure to clear the snow from plaintiff's street was negligent.

> Defendant contends in his motion to dismiss that this Court lacks subject-matter jurisdiction over plaintiff's claim.

B. *State the Conclusion*

Immediately after identifying the target of your attack, you should state the ultimate conclusion of your argument. It is often helpful to add a very brief summary of the reasons you will advance in support of your conclusion.

If you have properly selected the target, your conclusion should be simply that the targeted position of your opponent is wrong, or that your opponent's targeted actions were illegal. The statement of the conclusion can be as simple as "Plaintiff's argument is incorrect," or as complex as: "Plaintiff's argument is incorrect for three reasons: first, . . . ; second, . . . ; and third, ..."

Here are the set-up examples given above, but with conclusions appended:

> On October 10, 1991, defendant informed plaintiff that it would not make payment under the terms of the June 15, 1991 contract. This announcement constituted an illegal breach of contract for which plaintiff is entitled to compensation.

> Plaintiff alleges in Count One of the complaint that the city's failure to clear the snow from plaintiff's street was negligent. Plaintiff's allegation is incorrect because the city is under no duty to clear snow from local streets.

> Defendant contends in its motion to dismiss that this Court lacks subject-matter jurisdiction over plaintiff's claim. Defendant's motion must be denied for two reasons. First, plaintiff's claim presents a federal question under the Federal Tort Claims Act (FTCA) over which the Court has jurisdiction under 28 U.S.C. § 1346(b). Second, defendant's actions fall well outside the FTCA's discretionary function exception.

Note how the identification of the target combined with a statement of the conclusion provides the court with a sort of roadmap with which to follow the course of the ensuing argument. Needless to say, the ensuing argument should stick closely to this roadmap. If you find yourself straying in the body of the argument from what you promised to deliver in the set-up, go back and revise the set-up so that it previews the argument you actually present.

§9.2.2. Setting Out the Law.

With the set-up accomplished, we now proceed to the argument itself. Here we can begin to draw upon the syllogisms that underlie the argument and to integrate them into the written product.

A. *Identify and Introduce the Relevant Doctrine or Provision*

For the sake of clarity, the argument proper should begin by introducing the court to the important legal doctrines or constitutional or statutory provisions at issue. This part of the argument serves as a sort of *dramatis personae* – it tells the court what characters it can expect to encounter as the legal story unfolds. The introduction of the law in this part of the argument usually corresponds to the major premise of the underlying syllogistic legal argument.

Here are some examples of introducing the relevant law:

> The First Amendment of the United States Constitution provides: "Congress shall make no law . . . abridging the freedom of speech . . . ."

> Under the doctrine of strict liability, a person is liable for harm caused by dangerous activities even if that person was not negligent.

Federal question jurisdiction under 28 U.S.C. § 1331 extends to all civil actions arising under the constitution, laws, or treaties of the United States.

B. *Explicate the Law*

Few writing practices can so quickly confuse a reader as the use of terms that have been inadequately explained. The requirements of clear writing consequently dictate that once you have identified and introduced the relevant legal doctrines or provisions, you must explicate their meaning. That is, having introduced the characters in the story you are about to relate, you must tell the reader something about them.

In legal writing, explication of a legal doctrine or provision usually involves some discussion of its context and purpose. For example, a discussion of the context of a statutory provision might briefly touch on the nature of the enactment in which the provision is found (civil rights measure, public benefit program, etc.), the time of and historical reason for the legislature's enactment of the provision, and the role the provision plays in the larger statutory scheme. A discussion of the provision's purpose might add brief statements from the legislative history or from cases authoritatively interpreting the provision.

Your explication of the law in this part of the argument will usually be drawn from your grounding of the major premise of your syllogistic argument, and from grounded legal aspects of the minor premise. These elements should be woven together to create the smoothest possible legal discussion.

Below are two examples of explicating the law. Keep in mind that passages like these are not mere padding; they provide context necessary for an understanding of the ensuing argument and grounding for the premises on which you ultimately rely.

> The class action is a procedural device of relatively recent vintage that allows large numbers of similar claims to be adjudicated in a single proceeding. Fed. R. Civ. P. 23. Although class actions instituted under Rule 23 can save time and money for courts and litigants alike, they pose certain risks that require their use to be confined to a limited set of circumstances. *See id.,* Rule 23(b). The rule's drafters took special care to point out that the "difficulties which would be likely to arise if resort were had to separate actions" furnishes "the principal key" to the propriety of utilizing the class action device. Supplementary Note of Advisory Committee to Rule 23(b)(1) (1966).

> The first amendment's protection of freedom of speech is designed to assure that debate on public issues will be "uninhibited, robust, and wide-open." *New York Times Co. v. Sullivan.* The Court has suggested, perhaps somewhat inconsistently, that our national commitment to open debate stems from societal notions of both a "marketplace of ideas," *see Abrams v. United States* (Holmes, J., dissenting), and the need for intelligent self-government. *Sullivan.* In any event, as the Court has squarely held, "there is practically universal agreement" that a major purpose of the first amendment is to "protect the free discussion of governmental affairs." *Mills v. Alabama.*

C. *Set Out the Controlling Test, Step Analysis, or Factor Analysis*

The culmination of your discussion of the law should be the identification of the controlling test, step analysis, or factor analysis. This is the rule of law you are going to apply to the facts, and it should therefore precede as closely as possible the application portion of the argument. Examples of tests, step analyses, and factor analyses appear in § 5.4. This portion of your argument most often corresponds to the elaboration of a key legal term of the minor premise of your syllogistic argument.

§ 9.2.3. Apply the Law to the Facts.

Once you have set out the law and identified the relevant test, step analysis, or factor analysis, you must of course apply it to the facts. This part of the argument will be composed of your minor premise and its associated grounding.

As a rule, the application portion of the brief should mirror the structure of the test, step analysis, or factor analysis you are applying. For example, if you are using a three-prong test, you should apply each of the prongs in the same order in which the test lays them out. Similarly, if you are using a step analysis, you should follow the steps in order, discussing as necessary the facts relevant to each step.

The application portion of the brief is easiest to write when the minor premise of your argument, along with its grounding, is entirely factual. In such cases, the only real difficulty is deciding in what order to arrange the relevant facts to make the presentation as clear and easy to follow as possible.

The organizational difficulties increase substantially when the minor premise includes, as most do, a mixture of law and fact. Here, you must decide how to integrate two rather different types of discussions. The difficulty of this decision is compounded by the fact that a grounded complex minor premise actually consists of a series of elaborations of the law and applications of those elaborations to the facts. To do justice to these alternating elaborations and applications requires leaping from explications of the law to applications of law to fact, and back again – an awkward process in the best of circumstances.

In most cases, this organizational problem can be solved in one of two ways. The first way is to lump all the legal aspects of the grounded minor premise together and discuss them at the outset, followed by a discussion of all the factual aspects of the grounded minor premise. This approach has the advantage of concentrating the brief's legal discussions in a single location: a discussion of the legal aspects of the minor premise follows directly on the heels of the portion of the brief setting out the law to be applied (§ 9.2.2). The disadvantage is that the reader may forget the details of the law by the time he or she gets to the factual application, or may become confused as to which facts are relevant to what law.

The other possibility is to alternate brief discussions of legal aspects of the minor premise with brief applications of those legal aspects to the relevant facts. This approach has the advantage of clarifying the relevance of particular facts to particular law; its disadvantage is that discussions of the law are dispersed throughout the brief, making it harder for the reader to keep in mind the interrelationship of the various legal principles.

The following examples illustrate these alternative approaches. Both argue that a government policy of excluding women from active combat duty in the armed forces is unconstitutional on the ground that it fails the constitutional requirement that policies of gender discrimination be "substantially related" to an important governmental objective.

Example 1:
First Law, Then Application

A government policy is not "substantially related" to its objective if it is either overinclusive or underinclusive. *Craig v. Boren*. A policy of exclusion is overinclusive if it excludes those who ought not to be excluded. *Id.* A policy of exclusion is underinclusive if it fails to exclude those who ought to be excluded. *Id.*

A government policy of excluding women from active combat duty is both overinclusive and underinclusive. It is overinclusive because it excludes from combat duty a great many women who are entirely capable of effective military combat. The policy is also underinclusive because it fails to exclude from military service many men who are poor soldiers, yet who are nevertheless permitted to fill active combat roles.

Example 2:
Alternate Law and Application

A government policy is not "substantially related" to its objective if it is overinclusive. *Craig v. Boren*. A policy of exclusion is overinclusive if it excludes those who ought not to be excluded. *Id.* A government policy of excluding women from active combat duty is overinclusive. This is so because the policy unjustifiably excludes from combat duty a great many women who are entirely capable of effective military combat.

Similarly, a government policy is not "substantially related" to its objective if it is underinclusive. A policy of exclusion is underinclusive if it fails to exclude those who ought to be excluded. *Id.* A government policy of excluding women from active combat duty is underinclusive in addition to being overinclusive. The policy is underinclusive because it fails to exclude from military service many men who are poor soldiers, yet who are nevertheless permitted to fill active combat roles.

§9.2.4. Bolster With Analogous Precedent.

After setting out the law and applying it to the facts, the final step in the argument is to bolster your conclusion with analogous precedent, if any is available. Here and here alone is the place for an argument based on analogy (see §1.5) in which you describe the facts and the court's reasoning in some other case, and argue that the same result should be reached in the case at hand.

Note that the analogous precedent does not make the argument – the syllogism does that – but rather confirms the soundness of the syllogistic argument by showing that some other court has reasoned in just the way you ask the court to reason in this case. Bolstering a syllogistic argument with analogous precedent sends the court a message along the following lines: "Your Honor, I've set out the law for you and applied it to the facts, thereby demonstrating that judgment in favor of my client is compelled. But don't take my word for it – the Ninth Circuit said exactly the same thing in *Post v. Roberts*. Let me tell you about it. . . ."

§9.3. Clarity Always Takes Precedence.

One final warning is in order. Although the formula for writing an argument outlined above may provide useful guidance, it is only a guide; it is by no means a rigid set of commandments. The paramount consideration in all legal writing is clarity. If you can write an argument more clearly by departing from the formula, you should do so without hesitation.

§ 9.4. An Example of Reducing an Argument to Writing.

To illustrate the use of the briefwriting formula, let's reduce to writing the argument we constructed in Chapter 8 concerning the plaintiff who wanted to amend her complaint. We will first construct an outline using the formula set out in § 9.1, and then convert the outline into a complete written brief. Because a brief usually requires a bit more discussion than the logic of the underlying legal argument absolutely compels, additional research has been performed and is deployed in the outline and final product.

§ 9.4.1. The Outline.

Here is the formula for structuring a written legal argument. Elements of the argument have been added to the bare framework as appropriate, and are indicated by italics.

1. Set-up

   a. Identify your target
   – *plaintiff's motion to amend*

   b. State your conclusion
   – *plaintiff's motion should be denied*

2. Set out the law

   a. Identify and introduce relevant doctrines or provisions
   – *introduce Rule 15(a)*

b. Explicate the law (explain purpose, provide context)
   – *purpose is to facilitate decision on the merits,* Webb
   – *rule expresses general policy favoring granting of leave to amend,* Foman
   – *but there are certain circumstances where leave should be denied,* Foman
   – *courts should always consider prejudice to non-moving party,* Zenith

c. Set out the controlling test, step analysis, or factor analysis
   – *an untimely amendment should be denied where (1) no excuse for delay exists, and (2) the adverse party would suffer prejudice,* Manzoli

3. Apply the law to the facts

   a. First prong satisfied: plaintiff has offered no excuse
      – *no valid reason offered,* Hayes, *cf.* Island Creek

   b. Second prong satisfied: defendant would suffer prejudice
      – *would have to defend new claims after the close of discovery,* Hayes

4. Bolster with analogous precedent.
   – *discuss* Amendola.

§ 9.4.2. The Brief.

The brief on the following pages takes the set of nested syllogisms constructed in Chapter 8 and outlined in the preceding section, and converts them into a sustained written argument. The brief deploys all relevant research, including some additional research not specifically discussed in Chapter 8. Comments in the margin correlate different parts of the argument to the briefwriting formula and to the corresponding syllogistic premises. References to numbered syllogisms refer to the numbering in the diagram at the end of Chapter 8.

Set-up begins

Target identified

Conclusion stated

Rule 15(a) introduced

Brief explication of Rule 15(a).

Foman discussed as background

ARGUMENT

Three years after filing her original complaint and nearly two years after the completion of discovery, plaintiff moves the Court for leave to amend her complaint in order to add additional claims. Plaintiff's motion should be denied because allowing plaintiff to add entirely new claims at this late date would result in undue prejudice to the defendant.

Rule 15(a) of the Federal Rules of Civil Procedure provides:

> A party may amend the party's pleading once as a matter of course at any time before a responsive pleading is served. . . . Otherwise a party may amend the party's pleading only by leave of court . . . ; and leave shall be freely given when justice so requires.

The underlying purpose of Rule 15(a), like most other Federal Rules of Civil Procedure, is "to facilitate decision on the merits, rather than on the pleadings or technicalities." *United States v. Webb,* 655 F.2d 977, 979 (9th Cir. 1981); Fed. R. Civ. P. 1, 8(f). For this reason, Rule 15(a) expresses a general policy favoring the liberal granting of leave to amend. *Foman v. Davis,* 371 U.S. 178, 182 (1962).

Nevertheless, the Supreme Court has identified several circumstances in which leave to amend may properly be denied. These circumstances include: "undue delay, bad faith or dilatory motive on the part of the movant, repeated failure to cure deficiencies by amendments previously allowed, [and] undue prejudice to the opposing party by virtue of allowance of the

Note that all this background is designed primarily to provide context for the *Manzoli* test

amendment." *Id.*; *accord Riofrio Anda v. Ralston Purina Co.,* 959 F.2d 1149, 1154 (1st Cir. 1992). According to the Court, consideration of these factors is not optional: a court entertaining a Rule 15(a) motion to amend is "*required* to take into account any prejudice [the non-moving party] would have suffered as a result." *Zenith Radio Corp. v. Hazeltine Research, Inc.,* 401 U.S. 321, 331 (1971) (emphasis added).

Manzoli test set out (major premise of Syllogism 1)

The First Circuit has interpreted the Supreme Court's rulings under Rule 15(a) to require denial of a delayed motion to amend if two conditions are satisfied: "an untimely amendment request should be denied where... [1] no excuse for delay existed and... [2] the adverse party would suffer prejudice or substantial inconvenience." *Manzoli v. Commissioner of Internal Revenue,* 904 F.2d 101, 107 (1st Cir. 1990).

Minor premise of Syllogism 1 (conclusion on how test comes out here)

Here, the plaintiff has offered no excuse for waiting three years to amend the complaint, and the defendant will suffer substantial prejudice and inconvenience; consequently, plaintiff's motion should be denied.

Major premise of Syllogism 2

In cases such as this where "a considerable period of time has passed between the filing of the complaint and the motion to amend," the courts of this Circuit place the burden on the plaintiff to show a "'valid reason for his neglect and delay.'" *Hayes v. New England Millwork,* 602 F.2d 15, 19-20 (1st Cir. 1979), *quoting Freeman v. Continental Gin Co.,* 381 F.2d 459, 469 (5th Cir. 1967).

Minor premise of Syllogism 2

Plaintiff has entirely failed to carry that burden. Plaintiff's only explanation of her motion to amend is the following brief comment: "Further review of the law and facts shows that plaintiff has additional state law claims in fraud and breach of contract." Plaintiff's Motion to Amend Complaint at 1.

Syllogism 3

What plaintiff fails to explain is why these insights occurred to her more than three years after filing the initial complaint and some twenty months after the completion of discovery. Plaintiff does not contend, for example, that new evidence has only just come to light, *cf., e.g., Island Creek Coal Co. v. Lake Shore, Inc.*, 832 F.2d 274 (4th Cir. 1987) (last-minute discovery of new evidence justified otherwise untimely motion to amend), or even that new evidence came to light during the discovery conducted two years ago. *Cf. Matarazzo v. Friendly Ice Cream Co.*, 70 F.R.D. 556, 559 (E.D.N.Y. 1976) ("discovery often justifies a subsequent amendment to the complaint"). The most likely explanation is that plaintiff "simply allowed [her] case to lie fallow for more than two years." *Hayes*, 602 F.2d at 20. This is not an adequate excuse. *Id.*

Argument turns to second prong of *Manzoli* test

Major premise of Syllogism 4

Minor premise of Syllogism 4

In addition, granting plaintiff's motion would cause substantial prejudice to defendant. Such prejudice occurs any time a defendant is forced to create a "new record," *Manzoli*, 904 F.2d at 107, or, more specifically, when a defendant is forced to defend new claims after the close of discovery. *Hayes*, 602 F.2d at 20; *Isaac v. Harvard University*, 769 F.2d 817, 829 (1st Cir. 1985). This is precisely what defendant would have to do in this case were the Court to grant plaintiff's motion.

Premise further explained to avoid conclusory assertion

For three years, the only claim in this case was one alleging gender discrimination under Title VII. In all its efforts investigating the case, conducting legal research, and developing facts through discovery, defendant aimed exclusively at the question of discrimination. Plaintiff's fraud and breach of contract claims are entirely different: they arise under different laws, of a different jurisdiction, and rest upon entirely different facts.

Defendant would thus have to begin constructing its defense from scratch; it would have to perform new legal research, conduct new factual investigations, and, most burdensome of all, take new discovery. To expose defendant to this new and unexpected burden so long after the initiation of this case would be highly prejudicial and manifestly unjust, contrary to the express language of Rule 15(a).

Bolster with analogous precedent

In *Amendola v. Bayer,* 907 F.2d 760 (7th Cir. 1990), a virtually identical case, the Seventh Circuit upheld a trial court's denial of leave to amend a complaint. Denial was proper, the court held, for three reasons. First, the plaintiff did not move to amend until a substantial amount of time – some nineteen months – had elapsed after the substantial completion of discovery. Second, the claims that the plaintiff sought to add were based on facts that were entirely within the plaintiff's knowledge and control, and plaintiff's counsel thus had no good excuse for failing to know all the relevant facts. Third, allowing amendment would have required the defendant to take new discovery. *Id.* at 764.

Be sure to draw the factual comparisons explicitly when analogizing

Here, twenty months have elapsed since the completion of discovery, one more than in *Amendola.* The fraud and breach of contract claims that plaintiff seeks to add rely on facts within plaintiff's knowledge and control – for example, plaintiff's recollection and understanding of promises and representations that were made to her at the time of her hiring. Finally, addition of these claims would require defendant to take substantial additional discovery. Defendant's discovery throughout this case has been guided solely by the need to defend against a claim of discrimination. *See* Defendant's First and Second Sets of Interrogatories; Defendant's First and Second Requests for Production of Documents; Depositions of George E. Chamberlain, Clara D. Noyes, and Juan Andres; Defendant's Request for Admission. None of the information collected to date would be of any value in defending against the new claims plaintiff seeks to add.

Conclusion

Add pro forma conclusion

For the foregoing reasons, plaintiff's motion to amend the complaint should be denied.

PART III
ADDITIONAL CONSIDERATIONS

Chapter 10

SPECIAL PROBLEMS

§ 10.1. The Big Case.
§ 10.2. No Controlling Authority.
§ 10.2.1. The Nature of the Problem.
§ 10.2.2. Grounding the Argument in First Principles.
§ 10.2.3. Justice, Morality, and Policy.
§ 10.3. Balanced Legal Writing.

§ 10.1. The Big Case.

The method for constructing and writing a legal argument set out in Parts I and II works best for the ordinary case – one in which the argument must be stitched together from bits and pieces of several judicial decisions, all of which are relevant but none of which is decisive. Not every case, however, fits this mold. Once in a while, legal research discloses a "Big Case" – a binding decision of a higher court in which the facts are so similar and the holding so decisive that it completely controls the outcome of the case at hand.

When a Big Case dominates the legal landscape, you are better off deviating from the usual argument format in two ways. First, you should short-circuit the argument construction process and confront the Big Case immediately, without regard for the overall logic of the argument. A Big Case is to ordinary authority what an atomic bomb is to conventional warfare – nothing else really matters. To march carefully through a set of syllogisms, laying out a test in the abstract and applying it to the facts of the case along the way would be a waste of time; all concerned will only be waiting impatiently to learn your thoughts on the Big Case.

Second, you should construct an argument about the Big Case using analogies rather than syllogisms. There are only two arguments that a lawyer can make when confronted with a Big Case. If the holding of the Big Case favors your client, you must argue that the Big Case is exactly like the case at hand and its holding controls. If the holding of the Big Case favors your opponent, you must argue that the Big Case is distinguishable and has only minimal relevance or none at all.

This is probably the only occasion in legal argument when the use of bare analogical argument is desirable. These analogies, like all analogies, derive their persuasive force from an underlying syllogism (see § 1.5), and a Big Case is only a Big Case by virtue of the mutual agreement of the parties on an underlying syllogism concluding that the case is decisive if it applies. Because the parties by definition already agree on this unstated syllogism, the advocate need not state the syllogism explicitly, but may instead rely on it implicitly.

An argument relying on a Big Case is usually best written in the following form. First, introduce and describe the Big Case, discussing the facts, reasoning, and holding, as necessary. Try to avoid excessive description; you know you have gone too far if the reader can say: "By the time I finish reading this description, I could have read the case itself."

Second, argue that the case at hand is identical to the Big Case by demonstrating each salient similarity. Conclude by arguing that the court must reach the same result here. Only after the Big Case has been dealt with should you advance your other supporting arguments. Any such arguments should be presented in the usual syllogistic format.

If, in contrast, you are trying to escape the effects of a Big Case, you have two choices. If you are compelled to concede the impact of the Big Case, your only hope is to distinguish it. Such an argument would take exactly the same form as an argument relying on the Big Case, except that the argument would demonstrate the differences between the Big Case and your case rather than the similarities.

On the other hand, it is sometimes possible to argue that the Big Case is not really a Big Case at all – that is, to deny its "Bigness" by denying either its authority or its relevance. This approach generally calls for a different strategy. To begin an argument by distinguishing a case is to concede the force of that case. By dealing with the case immediately, you reveal that you think the case is one that *needs* to be confronted immediately – that it is, in other words, a Big Case.

Because you cannot both deny that a case is a Big Case and begin your argument by confronting it, you must downgrade your discussion of the alleged Big Case to the less prominent position you believe it ought to occupy. Thus, if you wish to deny the Bigness of the alleged Big Case, your best strategy is generally to proceed with the presentation of a normal syllogistic argument, discussing the alleged Big Case only at the point where it makes sense to do so within the syllogistic structure.

Of course, this strategy is risky and may backfire. If the court disagrees with you and decides that the Big Case is really Big, you are at a disadvantage because you have not thoroughly and forcefully dealt with the case. There is, unfortunately, no clean way out of this dilemma. Litigation, as we have seen, requires taking risks, and you can't hope to win unless you are willing to risk losing.

§ 10.2. No Controlling Authority.

§ 10.2.1. The Nature of the Problem.

At the opposite end of the spectrum from the Big Case is the problem of a complete lack of controlling authority. Suppose you research the law and find no controlling precedent on point. You expand your search and find that no court in any jurisdiction has ruled on the precise issue presented by your case. You expand your search again and find no decision by any court that seems to shed the slightest light on how your case ought to be decided. What do you do?

The most important point to keep in mind in this situation is that there really is no such thing as a complete lack of authority. American law is simply too well developed ever to present a situation in which no court has ever said anything of relevance to the resolution of a particular legal question. The problem in these cases is not that there is no relevant authority at all, but that the relevant authority seems too attenuated to be convincing – any guidance the existing decisions might provide seems too remote to serve as the grounding for a persuasive argument. The advocate's primary task, then, is to present the attenuated authority in as positive and persuasive a manner as possible.

§ 10.2.2. Grounding the Argument in First Principles.

One common way to present attenuated authority in a positive light is to "go back to first principles." In any given area of law, it is almost always possible to identify a handful of basic, foundational principles that courts treat as authoritative, and that they use as guideposts to orient themselves in complex cases. In federal civil procedure, for example, such principles might include the general preference for notice pleading, the avoidance of "traps for the unwary," and the fundamental power of the courts to act in the interests of justice. In contract law, courts often proceed from the principles that the parties are entitled to the benefit of their bargain, that unjust enrichment should be avoided, and that the offeror is master of the offer.

It can be tempting at times to treat these doctrines as cliches that lack any authoritative punch. This is usually a mistake. Although controlling authority explicitly deciding a legal question will always trump a general invocation of first principles, these doctrines are far from dead letters; what makes first principles seem like cliches is their widespread acceptance, not their entombment by later elaboration.

The advocate's strategy, then, should be to ground a standard syllogistic argument in first principles articulated by authoritative sources. For example, suppose you represent a person in an irreversible coma who, through her family, asserts a federal constitutional right to be removed from artificial life support. The Constitution obviously says nothing specific on the subject. Suppose further that no prior federal court decisions address the question. You might then build an argument by invoking constitutional first principles concerning individual liberty and autonomy, or the constitutional ordering of the relationship between the individual and the state. This is more or less what happened in *Cruzan v. Director, Missouri Department of Health,* the case in which the Supreme Court first addressed this issue.

Of course, the mere invocation of first principles does not amount to a complete argument; you must still indirectly ground your argument in the relevant first principles as persuasively as possible using the methods discussed in Chapters 4, 5 and 6. Linking the resolution of current, specific legal questions to remote first principles is not always easy. Sometimes the relevant first principles seem so distanced from the specific question at hand that one is hard put to argue persuasively that they provide any kind of useful guidance for resolving the question. Nevertheless, the advocate must show that some first principle supports the client's position, however weakly, because the alternative is to make no legal argument at all.

§ 10.2.3. Justice, Morality, and Policy.

When all else fails, the advocate may have no choice but to turn to general arguments based on justice, morality or policy. The appeal of such arguments is understandable enough: the law is supposed to be about justice and morality, so it seems only logical that arguments invoking those considerations would carry considerable weight. They do not. Indeed, such arguments are sometimes viewed within the legal system as the last refuge of scoundrels; they may be seen as a form of table-pounding to which lawyers resort when they have no "real" legal authority on which to rely.[7]

Nevertheless, if you cannot show that your position is legally right, you will have to show at least that it is morally or politically good. Such a showing is not enough by itself to win the case, but it might be enough to make the judge want to rule in your favor. Even if you yourself cannot find a clear legal path to success, a judge who wants badly enough to rule for you may be able to find a way to do so.

Keep in mind that the legal system's suspicion of arguments based on justice or policy does not mean that such arguments should always be avoided. It means only that such arguments should be advanced primarily to *supplement* sound legal arguments. The combination of a sound legal argument and an emotional appeal can be highly effective; it not only induces the court to want to rule in your favor, but also furnishes it with the tools to do so.

---

[7] One reason for this may be a systemic presumption that legal rules already embody society's notions of justice and sound policy. On this view, merely to apply legal rules is by definition to achieve justice and morality and to effectuate sound social policy. It follows that arguments to the contrary are properly addressed to legislatures, which have the power to alter legal rules, rather than courts, which exist only to apply them.

Rather, what the advocate should try to avoid is appeals to justice, morality and policy unsupported by any legal argument.

§ 10.3. Balanced Legal Writing.

Not all legal writing is advocacy. Sometimes lawyers are called upon to perform balanced analyses, avoiding position-driven posturing in favor of honest evaluations. A memorandum from an associate to a partner in a law firm is probably the most common example of this type of balanced legal writing.

The method we have developed for constructing legal arguments is equally applicable to balanced legal writing and advocacy. Balanced legal analysis differs from advocacy only in that it requires the construction of arguments on both sides of an issue instead of just one side. In order to perform a reasoned and informed analysis, a lawyer must be able to understand both sides of an issue and to discern the arguments that could be advanced for either side.

The writing of a legal memorandum also need not differ significantly from the writing of a brief. Most lawyers who request a balanced written analysis also want a conclusion, and a good memorandum will present one, however tentatively. In a sense, the memorandum is a piece of advocacy in which the writer supports his or her conclusion. A memorandum may discuss counter-arguments more deliberately and extensively than a brief, and it may advance arguments in a less aggressive tone, but a memorandum, like a brief, is still only a series of legal arguments linked together in service of an ultimate conclusion.

Chapter 11

RESPONDING TO ARGUMENTS

§ 11.1. Affirmative and Responsive Arguments.
§ 11.2. Treat Your Opponent's Arguments Respectfully.
§ 11.3. Three Ways to Respond.
  § 11.3.1. Denial.
  § 11.3.2. Shifting Ground: Confession and Avoidance.
  § 11.3.3. Ignoring Arguments.
§ 11.4. Organizing Responses.

§ 11.1. Affirmative and Responsive Arguments.

A lawyer's presentation in a case generally includes three conceptually distinct elements: the *case-in-chief,* the *response,* and the *rebuttal.* The case-in-chief consists of all the arguments and evidence necessary to tell a coherent story showing that your client is entitled to judgment. It is what the judge would see and hear if your opponent never showed up in court and you simply went ahead and put on your case without interruption or contradiction. Arguments made in support of a case-in-chief are thus *affirmative* arguments – they tell the court why your case-in-chief is good enough to win.

It is never strictly necessary for a lawyer to put on anything other than a case-in-chief. If your arguments are sound and your evidence persuasive, you might simply want to spin your tale and submit it to the decision maker. To do so is to tell the decision maker, in effect, "Look, I don't care what the other side says; I've told you my story and you can take it or leave it."

The problem with this approach, however, is that in most cases *both* sides are capable of mounting coherent, credible cases-in-chief. For example, consider a personal injury case arising out of an automobile accident at an intersection. The plaintiff says the light was red, and can produce two eyewitnesses to corroborate her story. The defendant says the light was green, and can also produce two eyewitnesses to say so. Assuming that all the witnesses are superficially credible, a jury would rule for the plaintiff if all it heard were her case-in-chief, and would rule for the defendant if all it heard were his case-in-chief.

What happens in real cases is that the jury hears both cases-in-chief and must then decide which of these two internally consistent and well-documented stories is the more plausible. This is a situation that most advocates like to avoid, because it's a crapshoot; you can never be sure which of the two stories the jury will prefer. As a result, advocates almost universally try to strengthen their final position before the decision maker by supplementing their case-in-chief with a responsive case.

A responsive case consists of arguments and evidence showing that your opponent's case-in-chief is wrong. In the automobile collision case mentioned above, for example, a responsive case might consist of evidence and arguments showing that the testimony of your opponent's witnesses is not credible. Thus, you might try to show that a witness lacked a clear view of the traffic light, or has poor eyesight, or was looking at something else at the moment of the crash, or harbors a grudge against your client. Undermining your opponent's case-in-chief in this way leaves the jury, if all goes well, with only one plausible story to choose.

Finally, a rebuttal case consists of responses to the responses of your opponent. That is, rebuttal shows why your opponent's responses fail to undermine your case-in-chief. The three parts of a case – case-in-chief, response, and rebuttal – correspond roughly to the direct examination, cross-examination, and redirect examination of a witness. They also correspond roughly to the opening brief, response brief, and reply brief in the briefing and argument of a motion or appeal.

It is important to keep in mind that the division of a case into these parts is primarily conceptual, and that the same argument or piece of evidence can serve more than one function. For example, the defendant's testimony in an automobile accident case that the light was green is a critical part of the defendant's case-in-chief. But that same testimony also responds indirectly to the plaintiff's assertion that the light was red: the plaintiff says the light was red, but the light could not have been red because it was actually green. Similarly, the plaintiff's rebuttal of the defendant's attack on a witness' credibility may also support the case-in-chief by showing why the witness is worthy of the fact finder's trust.

§ 11.2. Treat Your Opponent's Arguments Respectfully.

A responsive argument is nothing more than a particular type of legal argument. Responses differ from other kinds of arguments not in their form – like any arguments, they should take the form of well-grounded syllogisms – but in their function. As we have seen, the primary function of a response is to undermine your opponent's arguments.

In order to undermine your opponent's arguments effectively, you must know precisely what they are. Even the most elegant and powerful argument is useless if it is deployed against the wrong target. Your arguments must actually respond to the arguments made by your opponent if they are to do any real damage.

For this reason, the first step in the formulation of a response always is to carefully and respectfully scrutinize your opponent's arguments for the purpose of identifying the real targets of your attack. Indeed, you should try to break down your opponent's arguments into their constituent syllogisms to find out exactly how the arguments are constructed and grounded.

It is sometimes tempting to treat your opponent's arguments cavalierly, particularly if the briefs are poorly written or organized, or the arguments seem intuitively weak. Nevertheless, the time invested in critical analysis of your opponent's argument is time well spent. It will do you no good to demolish straw men of your own creation; you must be sure to demolish the real thing.

§ 11.3. Three Ways to Respond.

When you have identified your opponent's arguments you are ready to map out a strategy for responding to them. There are three basic ways to respond to any argument: you can deny the argument outright; you can shift ground through the tactic of confession and avoidance; or you can ignore the argument entirely.

§ 11.3.1. Denial.

The strongest type of response by far is denial. A denial meets an argument head on; it says bluntly "you are wrong." Because even erroneous arguments usually rest on internally consistent syllogisms, the most common way to deny an argument is to deny one or both of the premises upon which it rests. Such a denial can be constructed by the following method:

1. identify the erroneous premise;
2. reformulate the premise correctly;
3. ground the reformulated premise.

For example, suppose your opponent argues that Socrates is immortal. After studying your opponent's argument, you decide that the argument is based on the following syllogism:

1. All men are immortal.
2. Socrates is a man.
3. Therefore Socrates is immortal.

Your response would probably go like this. First, you would decide to respond to this argument by denying its major premise; the premise is wrong: all men are mortal, not immortal. Second, you would substitute the properly formulated major premise:

1. All men are mortal.

Finally, you would ground this premise in the usual way, either directly through citation to authority or evidence, or indirectly by making it the conclusion of a different grounded syllogism. For example:

1. All men are mortal. Affidavit of Hippocrates, M.D., ¶ 3.

Such an argument could be incorporated into a brief in several ways. Here is one example:

> The key to defendant's argument is his claim that all men are immortal. Defendant is incorrect. In fact, quite the opposite is true: all men are mortal. In his affidavit, Dr. Hippocrates addresses precisely this point. According to Hippocrates, "as far as medical science is aware, no person has ever lived more than 120 or so years, and the actual figure is probably lower." Hippocrates Affidavit, ¶ 3. Immortality, he goes on, is "incompatible with human physiology." *Id.*, ¶ 4.

In a legal context, advocates most commonly deny the premises of their opponents' arguments because they deny that some case or statute says what their opponent claims it says, or because they deny that the evidence shows what their opponent claims it shows.

Although less common, the conclusion of a syllogism may also be denied on the ground that it does not follow from the syllogism's premises – in other words, the syllogism is improperly constructed. For example, suppose your opponent challenged the constitutionality of a law by advancing the following argument.

1. The first amendment prohibits abridgement of the freedom of speech.
2. This law takes plaintiff's property without just compensation.
3. Therefore this law violates the first amendment.

Regardless of the truth of these propositions, the syllogism is vulnerable to attack on the grounds that the premises do not match, and, therefore, the conclusion does not follow from the premises: a taking without just compensation violates the fifth amendment, not the first.

In these situations, the best strategy is to lay bare the structure of your opponent's argument for the court and point out the fallacious reasoning.

> Plaintiff spends a good fifteen pages of her brief arguing that the challenged law violates the first amendment, but her reasoning seems rather confused. Plaintiff argues at length that the statute takes her property without just compensation, but this claim is completely irrelevant to the constitutionality of the statute under the first amendment. In order to make out a violation of the first amendment, plaintiff would have to show that the law somehow abridges her freedom of speech. U.S. Const. amend. I. But the taking

of property, with or without compensation, in no way limits plaintiff's ability to speak or write freely. *Cf. id.*, amend. V.

§ 11.3.2. Shifting Ground: Confession and Avoidance.

A second way to respond to an opponent's argument is to change the subject. Such a response does not confront the opposing argument head on by denying it, but instead suggests that the opposing argument requires no response because it is unimportant to the resolution of the case. This strategy is sometimes known as *confession and avoidance.*

An advocate who denies an opponent's argument in effect concedes, at least provisionally, that the opponent has addressed a subject relevant to the ultimate outcome of the case. By undertaking the effort necessary to mount a convincing denial, the advocate implies that the opponent's argument is one that deserves a response – it is an argument that can do some damage to the advocate's position if not turned aside by a competent denial.

The confession and avoidance strategy takes a different approach. Rather than respond directly to an opposing argument, an advocate using this tactic shifts ground to a different subject altogether. Instead of denying the opposing argument by saying "you're wrong," the advocate effectively says, "even if you're right it doesn't matter – I still win." The advocate thereby takes the position that the opponent's argument, even if correct, is harmless because the opponent is simply arguing about the wrong issue. Confession and avoidance says to the court: "There's no point wasting time on these arguments because they're irrelevant to the resolution of this case. Let's talk about what's really important here."

This type of response comes up in several contexts. A motion to dismiss, for example, is by definition a form of confession and avoidance because the allegations of the complaint must be taken as true. Every motion to dismiss says to the court: "These allegations might be true or they might be false, but it doesn't really matter because even if they're true the complaint must be dismissed." The ground-shifting nature of motions to dismiss gives them their exceptional strategic strength. The party moving to dismiss is able to say, in essence: "I win this case under any set of circumstances you can name. Naturally, I win if the allegations of the complaint are false, but I also win if the allegations are true."

Jurisdictional arguments are common subjects for confession and avoidance: "Plaintiff argues that defendant violated plaintiff's constitutional rights. The court, however, need not reach this issue because it lacks jurisdiction to hear the case." Use of an affirmative defense likewise shifts the ground of discussion: "It makes no difference if the parties had a contract or not, because even if they had a contract it would be unenforceable as contrary to public policy." Many *fallback* arguments – those to which the advocate retreats if the court rejects a leadoff argument – also take the form of confession and avoidance: "First, you're wrong; second, even if you're right, it doesn't matter."[8]

Note that ground-shifting responses must be constructed independently of your opponent's arguments – unlike denials, they cannot be piggy-backed on your opponent's syllogisms. This is because a ground-shifting response is in a sense not a response at all. Confession and avoidance leaves your opponent's arguments standing; it merely shifts

---

[8]The fallback argument need not always be the ground-shifting argument. One could also argue: "First, it doesn't matter whether you're right or wrong. Second, even if it does matter, you're wrong."

the court's attention to some other issue that you contend is more important. Thus, you must construct a ground-shifting argument just as you would construct an affirmative argument to support your case-in-chief – by fashioning a syllogistic argument and grounding its premises.

§ 11.3.3. Ignoring Arguments.

The final way to respond to an argument is to ignore it entirely. Not every argument deserves a response. Some arguments are so weak or so obviously irrelevant that the advocate need not bother pointing out their flaws to the court. Moreover, the advocate may not always have the space to respond to each and every argument made by the opponent. Most courts impose page limits on briefs, so advocates frequently are physically unable to respond to every point raised by their opponents. In such cases, the advocate has no choice but to ignore some arguments.

Not all arguments, however, are equally good candidates for the cold shoulder treatment. There are two ways to win a case. One way is to present a better argument than your opponent and persuade the judge of your position. The other way is to make an argument that the other side fails to dispute.

In theory, no case should ever be decided merely because some legal argument goes undisputed. Every judicial ruling must be consistent with the law, and a court therefore should never fail to satisfy itself that its ruling will be legally correct. Normally, courts rely on the parties to brief competing sides of the relevant legal issues. But even if one party fails to do an adequate job of briefing its side of a legal issue, a court should never take the word of the other party merely because its word has not been effectively disputed. Rather, the court should undertake its own legal research to make sure that its ruling will be lawful. In practice, however, courts rarely undertake significant independent legal research. As a result, courts often accept undisputed arguments simply because they are undisputed.

This fact of legal life means two things for advocates. First, the advocate should try to respond to all non-frivolous arguments whenever space permits, even if only in a footnote. Second, the advocate should always at a minimum respond to any *dispositive* opposing argument – one that, if left undisputed, will entitle the opponent to victory. Where an opponent's argument is necessary for victory but is not by itself sufficient for victory, the advocate has more discretion about whether to respond.

Finally, it is worth bearing in mind that lawyers can be competitive, and they sometimes find it easy to get into slugfests with their opponents in which each and every point made by the other side prompts a massive counterattack. The goal of advocacy, however, is simply to win your case, not to gratify your ego by crushing an opponent.

§ 11.4. Organizing Responses.

Responses often present difficult organizational choices. For example, a response brief is the forum not only for responding to the other side's arguments but for presenting affirmative arguments on behalf of your client as well. The advocate must decide how much space to allocate to each portion of the presentation, as well as the order in which to present the various arguments.

The cardinal rule for organizing any kind of response is *never let your opponent set your agenda.* Suppose you receive your opponent's opening brief. The brief has three sections, each making a different argument. It may be tempting to draft a response brief organized in a parallel format – your first section responds to your opponent's first section, your second section responds to your opponent's second section, and so on. To do so is to play into your opponent's hands.

The order in which arguments are presented can greatly influence their persuasiveness. Your opponent will inevitably choose to present arguments in an order favorable to his or her success, not yours. You must do the same. Start your brief with whatever argument is strongest for you, not for your opponent, and organize any direct responses to your opponent's arguments in the same way. You should not abdicate control over the order of presentation to your opponent merely because he or she had the opportunity to fire the first shot.

Remember also that you can almost never win a civil case merely by poking holes in your opponent's arguments. In order to win, you must present a strong case-in-chief. Accordingly, responses should always take a back seat to the presentation of affirmative arguments. Only after you have put on the best possible case-in-chief should you attempt to respond to your opponent's arguments.

When both parties stick to their own game plans, the result can sometimes be a pair of briefs that seem for the most part to argue past one another without really joining issue. This is often a sign of the strength of the advocacy, not its weakness. Although it is usually a bad idea to make no response at all to your opponent's brief, there is nothing wrong with crafting a brief that creates the general impression that your opponent has not addressed any of the really important issues. In any event, this is certainly preferable to creating the impression that your opponent has identified all the important issues and all you can do is respond as best you can.

Chapter 12

SOME COMMON RHETORICAL TECHNIQUES

§ 12.1. The "Shared Struggle."
§ 12.2. Use the Language of Fallback Arguments.
§ 12.3. The Persuasiveness of Detail.
§ 12.4. Attack the Opponent, Not the Court.
§ 12.5. Calling Attention to the Legal Standard.
§ 12.6. Providing the Court With Escape Routes.

When crafting arguments, the advocate should never forget that the most important weapon by far in the battle to persuade is clarity. An unclear argument or an obscure brief will never persuade anyone because it cannot be understood. Arguments should also be well-organized, and the advocate should take pains to make the organization clear to the audience so that it can more easily follow the presentation. The language used should of course be as clear and simple as possible.

Apart from writing and arguing clearly, lawyers commonly use a variety of rhetorical techniques to enhance the persuasiveness of their advocacy. This chapter examines a few of these techniques.

§ 12.1. The "Shared Struggle."

As a rule, advocates should never acknowledge uncertainty in the law. For the advocate, the law is always crystal clear – and, of course, always clearly favorable to the client. As we have seen, advocates need to adopt this air of certainty in order to make persuasive arguments. You will hardly help your client's cause if you begin your argument by claiming that the law is confusing or ambiguous. If the law is ambiguous, then someone else's interpretation of the law might be as good as yours; and if someone else's interpretation is as good as yours, the court has no particularly compelling reason to rule for you instead of your opponent.

Once in a while, however, the law really is exceptionally ambiguous or confusing or difficult. In these relatively rare circumstances, an advocate would only undermine his or her credibility by claiming that the law is crystal clear; to make such a claim would suggest that the advocate either cannot recognize a genuinely difficult area of law when he or she sees one, or is so committed to posturing and bluffing that he or she is unlikely to be helpful to the court in its attempts to understand the case.

In such a situation, an advocate may depart from the usual rule of claiming legal certainty and instead attempt to engage the court in a "shared struggle" to understand the law. Here, the advocate frankly acknowledges the ambiguity or difficulty of the law and casts the argument as one in which the court and the advocate, working together as partners, will try to make sense of it. The shared struggle approach usually goes something like this:

> Unfortunately, the Supreme Court has provided little concrete guidance to the lower courts in this area. Although the Court routinely purports to rely on its holding in *Roberts,* this holding is difficult to square with the Court's more recent rulings in *Smith* and *Thomas.* Indeed, the Seventh Circuit has called the *Roberts* and *Thomas* cases "flatly inconsistent." *Upton v. Vinci.* To complicate matters even further, the Court's decision last term in *West* produced four separate opinions with no clear majority on any single issue.
>
> Despite the relative disorder of the law in this area, it is nonetheless possible to identify at least a few points on which the Court seems consistently to agree . . . .

Of course, it always happens that this arduous labor results in an interpretation favorable to the client. Still, the advocate's position somehow seems more credible when it is derived in this superficially more honest and sincere way.

§ 12.2. Use The Language of Fallback Arguments.

As we have seen (§ 11.3.2), fallback arguments are those to which the advocate retreats in the event that the court rejects a previously advanced argument. Although fallbacks are often associated with the responsive tactic of confession and avoidance – "I win because you're wrong, but even if you're right, I still win" – they can also be used to organize affirmative arguments. For example, one can argue: "I win for reason X. But even if I don't win for reason X, I still win for reason Y."

You should organize your arguments into leadoffs and fallbacks whenever possible. First, organizing your arguments in this way brings conceptual order to your presentation. It tells the court how each argument relates to every other argument, and what the effect on the outcome of the case will be should the court adopt or reject any particular argument. Second, organizing your arguments into successive fallbacks gives the court a methodology for deciding the case. The court need not figure out for itself how to navigate through the conceptual thickets of the arguments; all it has to do is follow your step-by-step instructions.

You can most clearly signal the introduction of a fallback argument by using the words "even if... still." For example:

> Even if the court has subject-matter jurisdiction, the case still must be dismissed for failure to state a claim upon which relief can be granted.

> Even if the statement is hearsay, it is still admissible under the exception for excited utterances.
>
> Even if the statute does not violate the first amendment, it must still be struck down because it takes private property without just compensation in violation of the fifth amendment.
>
> Even if the transfer constitutes "income" within the meaning of the Internal Revenue Code, it is still not subject to federal tax because it is deductible.

Of course, like anything else, fallback language should not be used to the point where it becomes numbingly repetitive. Where two arguments merely advance alternative grounds for reaching the same result, it is permissible to couch them as alternatives:

> This case must also be dismissed because . . . .
>
> This evidence also must be admitted because . . . .
>
> The statute is also unconstitutional under . . . .

§ 12.3. The Persuasiveness of Detail.

Here is an account of an event:

> Yesterday, on my way home from work, I saw a UFO.

Here is another account of the same event:

> Yesterday I left work as I usually do about 5:30 p.m., and drove home following my normal route. Just as I pulled out from West Road onto Route 137, I noticed a reddish light low on the horizon. As I approached the WVPR transmission antenna, I could see that the

> object, which I assumed to be a small plane, seemed to be flying lower than the top of the antenna. I thought that was strange, because there are no air fields anywhere nearby, and I thought perhaps the plane might be in trouble. As I drove closer, though, I saw that the light was hovering, really – not moving at all. And then I saw that what I had taken to be a single reddish light was actually a series of alternating yellow and red lights....

You can imagine the rest.

No matter what you may think about the existence of UFOs, there can be no question that the second account is more persuasive than the first. The reason is *detail* – the more detailed the account, the more likely we are to believe it. For some reason, a detailed story is more persuasive, even when the speaker is trying to persuade us of something we might find inherently implausible.

The advocate can exploit this phenomenon by taking care to provide enough detail in any factual narrative to make it persuasive and interesting. Of course, the rules of good storytelling apply to legal factual narratives as much as to any other kind, and no narrative should be so detailed that it becomes tedious. But it is usually a mistake to edit facts down to the absolute minimum necessary for comprehension: you want the court to do more than understand the relevant facts; you want the court to believe them.

§ 12.4. Attack the Opponent, Not the Court.

Advocates frequently must criticize the rulings of courts. In every appeal, for example, at least one party argues that the lower court seriously erred. It is tempting in these situations to blast away with both barrels at the lower court or even to ridicule its rulings. Such attacks should be avoided.

Judges are members of a small, elite group. They often know each other, especially within a particular jurisdiction. The appellate judge sitting on the panel hearing your appeal may well lunch regularly with the trial judge whose opinion you are appealing. Even when judges don't know one another personally, they tend to look out for one another's interests. All this means that judges do not like to hear their fellows insulted, and the advocate would do well to tread lightly and respectfully in this area.

This does not mean, however, that advocates can never mount attacks on courts or judges; it merely means that such attacks must be disguised. The most common way to disguise an attack on a judicial ruling is to couch it as an attack on an opponent. In any kind of litigation, the parties routinely attack each other; such attacks are an expected and even indispensable feature of the adversary system. To attack a judicial ruling, then, one merely takes the arguments made by the court; attributes them, accurately or not, to one's opponent; and then takes one's best shots.

At no time, however, should any attack, even on an opponent, cross the boundaries of professional decency. There is an important difference between calling your opponents wrong and calling them stupid. Even the strongest arguments should be mounted against your opponents' arguments, not their character or intelligence.

§ 12.5. Calling Attention to the Legal Standard.

To prevail in a lawsuit, a party generally must show that it has satisfied some sort of legal standard – some test must be passed, some burden of proof or persuasion must be carried, or some presumption must be overcome. To win a case, an advocate must of course take the position that his or her client has satisfied the applicable legal standard. Conversely, the advocate must also argue that his or her opponent has failed to satisfy whatever legal standard might entitle the opponent to victory. Thus, the advocate must usually maintain the dual position, "we succeed and they fail."

This position is not as symmetrical as it might seem, however, because not all legal standards are equally easy to satisfy. Some legal tests consist of a single element, while others have multiple prongs. Some multi-prong tests are conjunctive – satisfaction of all prongs is necessary to pass the test – and some are disjunctive – satisfaction of one prong is sufficient to pass the test. Presumptions can run in favor of one side and not the other, and burdens can fall unequally on the litigants depending on their alignment.

As an advocate, you can sometimes exploit these disparities. Because you must convince the court that you win and your opponent loses, it is always in your interest to make your own legal standard seem as easy as possible to satisfy, and your opponent's legal standard seem very difficult to satisfy. Thus, it is often worthwhile to call the court's attention to the fact that your opponent has a difficult test to satisfy or a heavy burden to carry, or that your own test is easily satisfied or that an important presumption runs in your favor.

For example, suppose your opponent must satisfy a multi-prong conjunctive test in order to maintain the lawsuit. This is a difficult enough task, but you can stack the deck further in your favor by reminding the court just how difficult your opponent's task is:

> In order to have standing to sue in a federal court, a plaintiff must demonstrate that it has suffered a concrete injury, that this injury is traceable to the acts of the defendant, and that the injury is one that the

> court is capable of redressing. *Allen v. Wright.* The burden of showing each of these elements rests on the plaintiff. *Valley Forge Christian College.* Moreover, the plaintiff's failure to demonstrate even one of these three factors completely bars the court's exercise of jurisdiction and requires the court to dismiss the case. *Id.* Here, the case must be dismissed because the plaintiff fails to satisfy not one, but all three of these vital elements.

Conversely, you can also benefit from calling attention to your own legal standard when it is comparatively easy to meet:

> Under the Federal Rules of Evidence, admissions of a party-opponent are not considered hearsay and are therefore admissible. A statement can qualify as the admission of a party-opponent within the meaning of Rule 801(d)(2) in five entirely different ways. If the statement satisfies the conditions of even one subsection of Rule 801(d)(2), the court has no choice but to admit the evidence. Here, the statement at issue constitutes an admission of a party-opponent under two of the Rule's subsections.

> On this appeal, the factual findings of the trial court can be overturned only if "clearly erroneous." As this court has observed, the clearly erroneous standard is "highly deferential." *Babbitt v. Cole.* When applying the standard, the court may not "substitute its judgment for that of the trial judge, who was in a unique position to assess the facts." *Id.* Indeed, the court may reverse the factual findings of the trial court only if "no reasonable mind could view the evidence as supporting the conclusion reached by the factfinder." *Dierdorff v.*

Ellison. In this case, the factual findings of the trial court must be sustained. A reasonable mind not only could view the evidence as the trial judge did, but is virtually compelled to reach the same conclusion.

§ 12.6. Providing the Court With Escape Routes.

Judges tend to be extremely conservative. They dislike controversy and complexity. The ideal case for most judges is a routine case: the law is clear and well-established, the facts are beyond serious dispute, the outcome is obvious, and the possibility of reversal is nil.

Not every case, of course, is routine. Some cases present novel or exceedingly complex questions of law to which the answer is far from clear. Others may present legal or factual disputes the resolution of which will inevitably generate public controversy, sometimes regardless of how the court resolves the dispute. Most judges hate cases like this, and will go to some lengths to avoid placing themselves at the center of a controversy if they can. It follows that you can do the judge and your client a big favor in a complex or controversial case by providing the court with some avenue by which to avoid the most difficult or controversial aspects of the case.

Most difficult or controversial judicial questions arise on the merits of a dispute. In such cases, you can provide the court with an escape route by giving it some way to avoid reaching the merits. One way to do this is to show the court how it can rule in your favor on jurisdictional grounds – for example, the statute of limitations has expired, the plaintiff lacks standing, the case is not ripe, or the court lacks subject-matter jurisdiction.

Some of the most complicated and controversial legal questions arise under the Constitution. A time-honored rule of adjudication holds that a court should avoid constitutional questions if it is possible to decide the case on statutory grounds. Thus, you can provide the court with a way to avoid deciding a constitutional issue if you can show it how to rule in your favor under some statutory provision. For example, you might want to frame your argument like this: first, the government misapplied the relevant statute; second, even if it applied the statute correctly, the statute is unconstitutional. If the constitutional question is the kind that the judge wishes to avoid, your statutory argument may now look even more attractive to the judge than if you had raised it alone.

In an appeal, you can provide another kind of escape route by showing the court how it can remand the case without deciding the difficult merits issues. Perhaps some procedural error could be corrected, or additional facts need to be gathered at trial, or the case must be sent back so that the trial court can correctly apply the legal standard it said it was applying regardless of whether that standard is ultimately the proper one. It is thus usually wise to consider some satisfactory basis for remand even if you are asking the appellate court primarily for outright reversal of the lower court decision.

Keep in mind that you are never required to provide these kinds of escape routes. If the purpose of your litigation is precisely to obtain a novel constitutional ruling, you might even consider stripping away other potential arguments in order to paint the court into a corner where it cannot avoid reaching the issue you want it to reach. Even then, courts can be slippery, and you might find the court creating its own escape route in order to avoid controversy.

Chapter 13

THE ETHICAL LIMITS OF ARGUMENT

§ 13.1. The Ethical Dilemma.
§ 13.2. Official Constraints.
§ 13.3. Good Faith.
  § 13.3.1. Bad Faith: It's False.
  § 13.3.2. Bad Faith: No One Could Believe It.
  § 13.3.3. Good Faith: Winners and Losers.
  § 13.3.4. Maintaining Your Sense of Good Faith.
§ 13.4. The Settlement Option.

§ 13.1. The Ethical Dilemma.

Throughout this book we have spoken as though the making of certain legal arguments at certain times is mandatory. Your alignment, we have said, establishes your position, and your position dictates the content of your arguments. We have seen that a lawyer often has no real discretion: if you want to win your case you must make this or that argument, or you must respond to this or that argument of your opponent.

Yet lawyers are not free to make any argument at all just because doing so will help them win. Our justice system imposes many responsibilities on lawyers besides the duty to attempt to win cases. Lawyers are officers of the courts, citizens subject to the law, and human beings with ethical obligations to themselves and to others.

In most cases, a lawyer's legal and ethical responsibilities will not conflict with his or her responsibility to advance the best possible case on the client's behalf. Occasionally, however, a conflict may arise. When it does, a lawyer's legal or ethical duties may well preclude him or her from making strategically desirable, or even crucial, arguments.

Lawyers and courts have long struggled to identify the precise circumstances in which lawyers' ethical duties require them to refrain from making arguments that their syllogistic methodology tells them they should or must make in order to win their cases. Broadly speaking, three significant guideposts can help a lawyer decide whether to make a contemplated argument: the language of official constraints; the nature of good faith; and the lawyer's appreciation of the possibility of settlement.

§ 13.2. Official Constraints.

Most codes of professional responsibility require lawyers to represent their clients diligently and zealously. This requirement imposes upon lawyers an ethical duty to help their clients win cases. The lawyer is therefore generally bound to make those arguments that will help the client win.

On the other hand, legal and ethical codes explicitly restrict the types of arguments that lawyers can make. For example, Rule 11 of the Federal Rules of Civil Procedure requires that any pleading, motion or paper be "well grounded in fact" and "warranted by existing law or a good faith argument for the extension, modification, or reversal of existing law." The Rule also prohibits a lawyer from filing papers "for any improper purpose, such as to harass or to cause unnecessary delay or needless increase in the cost of litigation." Ethical codes generally impose similar restrictions, sometimes using the words "not frivolous" and "good faith" to describe the range of permissible arguments.

These requirements are easy enough to state, but notoriously difficult to apply. When is an argument "frivolous"? When is it "warranted" by the law? What does it mean for an argument to be "well grounded in fact"? Courts, no less than lawyers, have struggled, mostly unsuccessfully, to tease concrete guidance out of these vague terms.

Moreover, even if it were possible through diligent legal research to figure out precisely how litigation and disciplinary rules apply in particular situations, few lawyers would undertake the effort. In any given case a lawyer may face dozens, if not hundreds, of decisions that might implicate the rules. To research every potential ethical problem would slow the pace of litigation to a crawl and greatly multiply its cost. Consequently, lawyers must – and do – try to assure their own compliance with ethical constraints in less formal ways.

§ 13.3. Good Faith.

If there is any informal standard to which practicing lawyers commonly turn, it is the standard of "good faith." Good faith serves as a useful and reliable proxy for research into the nuances of ethical rules for three reasons. First, lawyers are required at all times to act in good faith under most disciplinary codes. Second, good faith is a common sense notion that can be assessed without time-consuming legal research. Third, lawyers can monitor their own good faith by simple reflection; it is a uniquely accessible yardstick.

But what does it mean to make a legal argument in good faith? The concept of good faith cannot easily be reduced to a formula; it is, rather, a bundle of related ideas that cluster around the notion of reasonable belief. In the context of mounting legal arguments, the inquiry into good faith centers on the following question: who, if anyone, could believe the arguments to be true? The less likely it is that reasonable lawyers and judges will believe your arguments, the less likely it is that your arguments satisfy the standards of good faith.

§ 13.3.1. Bad Faith: It's False.

A good way to begin to describe good faith is to consider its opposite, bad faith. The most egregious type of bad faith advocacy is to make an argument that you know to be false – to tell the litigation equivalent of a lie. To argue to the court that your client cannot move her neck when you know she can; to claim that a document sought in discovery does not exist when you know it does; to tell the court that a case says one thing when you know it says another – all these involve fundamental breaches of the duty to make arguments in good faith.

§ 13.3.2. Bad Faith: No One Could Believe It.

Sometimes, however, the truth can be difficult to ascertain. Evidence can be equivocal, and legal authority can be ambiguous. Perhaps the plaintiff looked both ways before crossing the street and perhaps not; perhaps a Supreme Court ruling means one thing, perhaps another. In these circumstances, you may disbelieve an argument but nevertheless be unable to "know" that the argument is false because the truth itself is debatable. These more common situations raise the question: can lawyers make arguments that they themselves disbelieve without breaching their duty to argue in good faith?

The answer is: it depends. The adversary system does not require lawyers to limit themselves to making arguments that they personally believe to be true. Clients are entitled to effective representation, and this may require lawyers to make arguments with which they disagree, and which they may even abhor.

The question is thus not whether you yourself believe the argument you wish to make, but whether the *judge* could believe it. If you think that an argument is so far from the truth as you conceive it that no reasonable judge could believe the argument – if you think, in other words, that the argument is frivolous – then you cannot make the argument in good faith. After all, if you believe that no reasonable judge could accept your argument, then the only reason to make the argument would be to try to sneak something past the judge – the essence of bad faith. Whenever you suspect that judicial acceptance of your argument depends on the stupidity or inattentiveness of the judge, you are probably acting in bad faith.

§ 13.3.3. Good Faith: Winners and Losers.

Although good faith forbids you to make arguments that you believe are so weak that nobody could possibly accept them, it by no means limits you to making only arguments that you genuinely think will persuade the court. No lawyer, no matter how experienced, can ever be sure what arguments will appeal to a court. As anyone who has spent even a few days in law school knows, courts often reach decisions that seem shockingly wrong, or that rely on the flimsiest reasoning. There is hardly a practitioner alive who has not been surprised by a court's rejection of an argument that he or she thought a sure winner, or its acceptance of an argument that he or she threw in as an afterthought. Furthermore, courts sometimes strike off on their own, relying on arguments that the parties did not brief and which the parties themselves may agree are wrong. Consequently, to require lawyers to make only what they believe to be winning arguments would impose an impossible burden on the successful practice of advocacy.

To be sure, it is always best to believe in the arguments you make. Advocates who believe that they are right can present their arguments with genuine passion and sincerity – which helps them persuade the court. But, although a belief in the power of your argument makes your advocacy more effective, it is not necessary for compliance with the duty of good faith.

§ 13.3.4. Maintaining Your Sense of Good Faith.

Distinguishing good faith from bad faith arguments requires the exercise of informed judgment, yet the objectivity necessary to make these judgments can be difficult to maintain. A lawyer's sense of good faith argument can be dulled from constant financial, professional, and personal pressures to win cases. The more deeply a lawyer becomes involved in representing a client, the more deeply he or she may become emotionally or intellectually attached to the client's cause. This type of attachment can greatly damage the lawyer's ability to remain objective about the validity of the arguments that will help the client win the case.

Even experience itself can be a mixed blessing. On the one hand, experience sharpens the judgment that lawyers need to distinguish accurately between those arguments that are sufficiently plausible to satisfy the duty of good faith, and those that are not. On the other hand, experience clouds that judgment by teaching the cynical view that virtually any argument stands a chance of acceptance given the right presentation and the right judge.

These threats to a lawyer's internal ethical compass pose real dangers: those who lose their way may incur discipline by state bars, the imposition of sanctions or fines by courts, and even criminal liability. It is therefore essential that lawyers make every effort to maintain their sense of good faith.

One way to retain perspective on the merits of a legal argument is to imagine yourself switching places with your opponent or with the judge. Ask yourself how you would react if you saw the contemplated argument in your side's brief. If you represented the other side, would you read the argument and begin to feel worried? Would you think the argument was one that required a serious rebuttal? If so, the argument can probably be made in good faith. Now suppose you were the judge. Would you take this argument seriously, and is there any chance that you would accept it? Or would you merely become annoyed at the party making the argument for wasting your time? If you cannot answer questions like these favorably, then you should drop the argument.[9]

§ 13.4. The Settlement Option.

The final factor in the good faith analysis is the possibility of settlement. Any case can be settled, and a lawyer's recognition of that fact can give him or her the sense of security necessary to refrain from making impossibly weak or frivolous arguments – no matter how necessary they may seem to be for victory.

It is also well to keep in mind that for every person who has been sued unjustly, ten more have been sued because they did something wrong. Our judicial system grants everyone the right to the best available representation, but – and it is often difficult for lawyers to admit this – those who break the law deserve to lose in court. It is part of a lawyer's job to recognize cases in which the clients' positions are untenable, and to tell those clients frankly that there is

---

[9] Some lawyers employ a very rough version of this analysis called, with tongue in cheek, the "laugh test." The laugh test works as follows. First, you imagine yourself making the argument to the judge. Next, you imagine the judge's reaction. If you visualize the judge bursting into laughter, then your argument fails the test and you should not make it. Of course, the laugh test catches only the worst arguments; there are many others that are too weak to make but that might not provoke gales of judicial mirth.

little that can be said on their behalf. Weak cases should be settled, and settled quickly.

Granted, it takes courage to confront clients with the weakness of their own cases. It takes even more courage to tell those clients that you insist they settle their cases, and it takes the most courage of all to tell them that you will be unable, in good faith, to make any decent arguments on their behalf should they be unwilling to reach a reasonable settlement. But the pain of confronting a client is probably slight compared to the pain of enduring the public humiliation of sanctions or bar discipline, and it is surely nothing compared to the private pain of knowing that you have compromised your principles and failed to do what you knew was right.

2470